# Reconnecting to the Earth

# Reclaiming Our Relationship to Nature and Ourselves

Aaron Hoopes

For permission, serialization, condensation, adaptions, or for our catalog of other publications, write to Ozark Mountain Publishing, Inc., P.O. Box 754, Huntsville, AR 72740, ATTN: Permissions Department.

The material in this book is intended for educational purposes only. No expressed or implied guarantee as to the effects of the use of the recommendations can be given nor liability taken. The publisher advises such activities as deep breathing, gentle movement, and meditation not be attempted or practiced without appropriate guidance and support.

Library of Congress Cataloging-in-Publication Data

Hoopes, Aaron  – 1963 -
*Reconnecting to the Earth* by Aaron Hoopes

Reconnecting to the Earth is a wake up call for anyone who is feeling that there is something not quite right with our world.

1. Spiritual   2. Earth  3.Reconnecting 4. Metaphysical
I. Hoopes, Aaron, 1963 - II. Metaphysical  III.. Spiritual   IV. Title

Library of Congress Catalog Card Number:2019938773
ISBN: 9781940265728


Title Page Image: DonkeyHotey/Flickr
Cover Art and Layout: Victoria Cooper Art
Book set in: Times New Roman, Georgia
Book Design: Tab Pillar
Published by:

PO Box 754, Huntsville, AR 72740
800-935-0045 or 479-738-2348; fax 479-738-2448
WWW.OZARKMT.COM

Printed in the United States of America

# Dedication

This book is respectfully dedicated to my dear friends Helen and Gregory Wilson, without whose inspiration it would never have existed.

# Acknowledgments

Thanks to my teachers Shanti Gowans, Chien "King" Lam, Takayuki Mikami, and Masatoshi Nakayama for their instruction and guidance on my path. Thanks to my parents, David and Kathleen, who encouraged me to follow this path and who spent many hours editing my books. Thanks to my Dragon Mountain Kung Fu students, who give me hope for the future. Thanks to Michael Denmeade, my brother on the journey. And a special thanks to Suzanne Lacey for her loving and caring support.

# Contents

# Author's Note

In this book I intend to take you on a journey of self-discovery. It is not always an easy path, but we have reached a point where action is required if we as a species are going to continue to live on this planet. I have no intention of talking about what's going to happen if you don't follow these practices or rehash the same old "fear porn" about how everyone's going to die if the whole world doesn't rally together. There is plenty of that out there already. The direction this book takes is toward something much more positive. This journey will take some discipline and integrity. There may be some difficulty and struggle along the way. However, as you reconnect with the Earth, you will feel the changes taking place within you . . . and *that* can change the world.

This book is separated into four sections. The first chapter is basically a wake-up call discussing the difficulties we are facing. It is a realistic assessment of our current situation and a vital first step on the path to reconnecting with the Earth. The second chapter provides a deeper understanding as to how we got into this predicament and the underlying framework of our society that has led us to this point. The third chapter is about changing the narrative we live in so that we can begin to shift our physical, mental, and spiritual beings toward a sustainable relationship with the Earth. The final chapter provides seven sets of seven fundamental guidelines for creating your own personal practice for reconnecting with nature, the Earth, and yourself.

If you are just beginning to become aware that there is something fundamentally wrong with what is happening to the planet, I recommend starting from the beginning to get the full picture. It may not be what you want to hear, but it is important to understand where we are starting from. If you have picked up this book because you are already aware of the huge problems we face as a society and civilization, I would recommend skimming the first two chapters and heading for the second half of the book. While the discussion of how bad things are cannot be left out, the exercises and practices for dealing with it are much more important to the process of reconnecting ourselves to the Earth.

~Aaron Hoopes 2019

# Introduction

*The first peace, which is most important, is that which comes within the souls of people when they realize their relationship, their oneness with the universe and all its power, and when they realize that at the center of the universe dwells the Great Spirit and that this center is really everywhere it is within each of us.*
*—Black Elk*

We stand on the threshold of a profound shift in our world. Our all-consuming industrial civilization has led us down a destructive path that has compromised our soil, food, water, and atmosphere. The drive for perpetual growth and profit has fractured the idea of community and instilled values of selfishness and personal gain in the people. It is now becoming apparent that our way of living has reached the point where going forward in the same manner is no longer feasible. The time has come to either do something different or face a bleak future of turmoil, war, and the breakdown of our way of life.

Fortunately, it appears that a growing sector of the population is finally starting to realize the degradation of the Earth can only be halted when the majority of people feel deeply that the Earth is sacred and that all living beings should be revered and cherished. The Earth has never been ours to ruin and destroy. As more and more people start to wake up to the understanding that what is happening to the Earth will affect us all, the need for a fundamental shift becomes imperative. An environmentally focused spiritual transformation is underway all over the planet. *Reconnecting to the Earth* is part of this process. It is now necessary that reverence for the Earth becomes a sacred calling for each of us. It is vital not only for the planet, but for the well-being of all beings living on it.

This book is for individuals who have begun to comprehend the extent to which we have damaged the Earth and have started to recognize the consequences for ourselves, for our society, and for all of life as we know it. It provides a framework for changing our way of relating to the natural world and enables us to reconnect with not only the Earth, but ourselves as well. It is a path that leads away from the darkness of the economic, social, moral, and environmental crises that is upon us and leads toward something deeply spiritual and fulfilling. It is vital that we quickly make a transition from exploitation and destruction to reverence and respect for the planet. This will not be easy. In fact, it is already too late for many species as it will soon be for a population that continues to insist on living unsustainably. However, as human beings, it behooves us to attempt to reclaim our souls and reconnect with the whole. Any other path only hastens our destruction.

*Most humans are alienated from their vital individuality—their souls—and humanity as a whole is largely alienated from the natural world that evolved us and sustains us. Soul has been demoted to a new-age spiritual fantasy or a missionary's booty, and nature has been treated, at best, as a postcard or a vacation backdrop or, more commonly, as a hardware store or refuse heap. Too many of us lack intimacy with the natural world and with our souls, and consequently we are doing untold damage to both.*
*—Bill Plotkin*

The simple truth is that we are no longer living in harmony with the natural environment. We have become disconnected, spiritually adrift in a dark and lonely world. Over time we have strayed from our path and gotten lost. The further we have strayed, the more distorted the path has become. And now we find ourselves hurrying to evolve spiritually before we plunge over the edge of a great chasm, a chasm we have created through our disrespect for the planet. Debating how we got to this point is irrelevant. This condition has come about through a centuries-long process that continues to accelerate. Being immersed in it, we hardly notice, but as the population of the planet increases exponentially, and the disasters multiply, the impending collapse gradually becomes more and more apparent. Soon it will overtake us.

*The most likely future will be battered by unstable climate and rising oceans due to anthropogenic climate change, stripped of most of the world's topsoil, natural resources, and ecosystems, strewn with the radioactive and chemical trash that our era produced in such abundance and couldn't be bothered to store safely.*
—*John Michael Greer*

We must do something different. We don't have the luxury of continuing to believe that technological advances make us more advanced. We cannot do whatever we want without care and ignore the consequences. We are not the masters of the Earth. The resources of the planet are not for us to use up at our discretion until they are gone. We are not supposed to callously dominate weaker species and subjugate everything else. No, we are simply part of the whole interconnected web of existence. Reconnecting with the Earth is a process of reestablishing an interconnected relationship with that whole. It is certainly a better path than the one we are on. Long ago, humans cultivated a relationship with spirit and practiced an underlying reverence for the life force that flowed through everything. The Lakota Sioux people pray and give reverence to *Wakantanka*, the Great Spirit or Creator that is a universal spiritual force that exists within all things. They believed Wakantanka was everywhere all the time and observed everything mankind did. This belief is present in many Native American cultures that see the idea of Great Spirit splitting itself up into everything—the stones, trees, animals, and tiny insects—making them all one. And in turn all these myriad of things that make up the universe flow back to their source, united in the one Great Spirit.

In ancient China it started with a man named Lao Tzu, the keeper of the Imperial Library. The story goes that Lao Tzu was well known for his wisdom, but became frustrated at the growing corruption of the government. He decided to give up his job to go live in the country. On his way out of the Imperial City, the guard at the gates asked him to write out the essence of his understanding to benefit future generations. Lao Tzu wrote the Tao Te Ching, left, and was never heard of again.

In the Tao Te Ching, Lao Tzu spoke of something undifferentiated and yet complete, which existed before Earth and the Heavens. He called it Tao. It is soundless and formless and depends on nothing. It does not change. It is everywhere. It is considered the mother of the universe.

Tao is a path of understanding and a way of being. It is a system of beliefs, attitudes, and practices set toward simply accepting yourself and the world. Tao teaches us to flow with life, live from our heart, and connect to the world in a way that helps us to learn more about ourselves and the world. It encourages us to drop expectations and live fully in the here and now. The Tao is the intuitive knowing through actual living experience of one's being. It is an active and holistic conception of Nature and the planet we live on. The Tao is ever-present, but must be manifested, cultivated, and/or perfected in order to be realized. It is the source of the universe, and the seed of its primordial purity resides in all things. Taoists let things achieve harmony on their own, according to their natural traits. It teaches us that we are a part of the planet as a whole, something we are in urgent need of relearning.

This book also incorporates the wisdom and knowledge of forward thinkers like Thomas Berry, a self-described Earth scholar and advocate of ecospirituality who proposed that a deep love and understanding of the history and functioning of the evolving universe is a necessary inspiration and guide for our own effective functioning as individuals and as a species. We need to embrace the common sense of what is right and wrong if we take our personal wants and desires out of the equation.

Today, many are rediscovering the joy and happiness that comes from being connected to the natural world. They are realizing the rich benefits from this path. A simple, yet profound, change is underway everywhere and shows that one individual can have an impact on the whole world.

You can make this change happen within you. It is an open door waiting for you to step through. By becoming aware of a few guiding principles that govern existence and by choosing to live in harmony with them, you can wake up to the natural world and experience the life-force energy that flows through all things and become part of something greater than yourself. Learn how to use all resources well, in a responsible and balanced way—for the elevation of every organism.

This is not some mystical power, nor is it a magic wand to solve all of your problems. Instead, it is a way of connecting to the world around you and realizing your role in maintaining it. To solve the problems facing the world we must step away from the seduction of the things that distract us and work together to bring balance to our world. It is time to wake up, strengthen the body, and clear the mind. There is much work to be done.

Come, walk with me.

# Chapter 1
# Wakeup Calling

## Wakeup Calling

*humanity rages*
*destruction in stages*
*of everything under the sun*

*the birds and the bees*
*the rivers and trees*
*it seems like the end has begun*

*a population of people*
*turned into sheeple*
*conditioned to crave more and more*

*life based on greed*
*want, desire and need*
*leads to nothing but war*

*the planet is dying*
*the animals crying*
*the forests all being cut down*

*the climate is hot*
*except when it's not*
*and some say we're all going to drown*

*we eat poison foods*
*take meds for our moods*
*we're so ill we cannot take action*

*to keep us asleep*
*the tendrils run deep*
*with all manner of lies and distraction*

*we cut the tops off the hills*
*down below oil spills*
*for us to progress, it is said*

*it's hard not to believe*
*if we do not grieve*
*soon we all will be dead*

*living in fear*
*something is near*
*now we are all scared to death*

*chaos and change*
*can often feel strange*
*please just take a deep breath*

*so what can we do*
*just me and you*
*to turn this whole thing around?*

*one way to recall*
*our connection to all*
*is to put our bare feet on the ground*

*now feel the Earth*
*remember its worth*
*let the energy run through your soul*

*look deep in your heart*
*that's where you start*
*to connect yourself to the whole*

*this cannot be solved*
*if you don't get involved*
*start now, there's no time to wait*

*change how you're living*
*stop taking, start giving*
*please, before it's too late*

*and so there you are*
*if you've made it this far*
*three last things I will say if I may*

*begin with a bow*
*stay here in the now*
*and remember to breathe every day*
*—Aaron Hoopes*

# A Different Path

*If people never experience nature and have negligible understanding of the services that nature provides, it is unlikely people will choose a sustainable future.*
*—Peter Kareiva*

Modern society acts as if the Earth and all its resources were ours to take, use, exploit, and discard. This process has been going on for quite a while, and accelerated significantly with the industrial revolution. For much of that time it was hidden from view mostly because the Earth is both enormous and incredibly resilient. It can take a lot of abuse before it starts to become noticeable. Unfortunately, we have now reached the point where it is no longer invisible, and daily it becomes more and more obvious that something is wrong. Our current way of life continues to hasten the process.

Did you ever have a thought deep in the back of your mind that there might be a better way of living than the way that is forced upon us by the hectic, stress-filled, technological, consumer society in which we live today? Alan Watts, the renowned Zen scholar, called that thought *hintegedanke*, which is a German word describing something just at the edge of consciousness. It is a hint of something greater, of some special connection we have with the world around us. For most, that feeling stays in the shadows of the mind as we drink our double lattés, drive our SUVs, text on our iPhones, and live our lives between the increasingly strident distractions that bombard us day and night.

What might this *hintegedanke* be trying to tell us?

Might it be offering to show us another way?

Might it be trying to remind us of something we have long forgotten?

Might it be presenting us with a different path to walk?

Is it quite possible that we have forgotten some very important knowledge over the past five thousand years, knowledge we were not supposed to forget? What can we do now that we find we are on the verge of collectively destroying ourselves?

Today we have too many choices, and the way forward seems more and more obscured. We have strayed from the path—not everyone, of course, and not all the time—but it is very easy to get caught up in the distractions and lose a sense of the self and a meaning of life when we are assaulted continuously by all manner of things vying for our attention.

It is time to walk a different path. This path is not about accumulating stuff. It's not about money and power. It's not about exploiting the natural world. It's not about dominating other living beings, and it has nothing to do with anger or hate. No, walking this path is simply about living, experiencing, and caring about this precious life and this abundant world. It is a holistic experience for the body, mind, and spirit. It is about recognizing, sensing, and exchanging energy with the natural world around us and feeling that energy reciprocated.

In the past, the lifestyles and belief systems of native tribes, indigenous people, and wise sages were a way of life that linked them to the natural world. By maintaining a connection to the natural order of things, it was possible to tap into the universal energy and live peacefully and in harmony with everything. Does that sound a bit exaggerated? Perhaps. It hardly seems possible that human beings could live like that from our present-day perspective. But, is it such an unrealistic goal to strive toward? What are the drawbacks of living a daily routine that is life-affirming and positive? If we take what we need from the Earth and give back to it in return in a sustainable manner, we become an integral part of the world we live in, not lords of creation. By supporting and caring for the world, the world supports and cares for us. By living and working in conscious, responsible, and wise ways we can exist in harmony with our environment.

Sadly, many of us have severed our connection to the natural world. We have become dependent on technology to make life easier, happier, and more fulfilling. We have become addicted to a host of things that keep us distracted, numb, and at odds with nature. And, while life may indeed seem, on the surface, to have become easier, happiness and fulfillment have proved elusive.

Instead of seeing ourselves as integral parts of the natural world—indeed, of the universe—we revel in accumulating stuff and feeding our desires. And, like any addiction, the more stuff we have, the more we need, until we become no more than the accumulation of all our stuff. We drive cars that burn our natural resources and destroy the atmosphere. We watch so much television that we are lucky most of us aren't brain dead. We use poisonous fertilizers to keep our lawns green and eat chemically or genetically altered food. We take pills for every problem this lifestyle has created and then take more pills for the problems that the first pills create. Other than a few domesticated species, our contact with the animals of the planet is primarily in zoos or on our plates at meal time, unrecognizable. And on top of it all, we are systematically destroying the oceans and forests that keep the Earth habitable.

*Arrested personal growth serves industrial growth. By suppressing the nature dimension of human development (through educational systems, social values, advertising, nature-eclipsing vocations and pastimes, city and suburb design, denatured medical and psychological practices, and other means), industrial growth society engenders an immature citizenry unable to imagine a life beyond consumerism and soul-suppressing jobs.*
—Bill Plotkin

In times like these, wise men and women come together. Along any journey it is useful to band together with like-minded people, especially when traveling through difficult terrain. Sharing knowledge and skills is vital for survival. But now it is even more important. It is the beginning of remembering what we have always known—we are inseparable from the laws of nature and the laws of the cosmos—and what goes around, comes back around. In banding together, each person imparts their wisdom like a piece in a great puzzle, which, when completed, creates a map showing the path forward. It is time for those who understand the difference between knowing the path and walking the path to walk it together.

This Earth is not much longer going to be content as humanity's captive. It is time for us to vibrate on a higher level, to connect with the divine that exists within us all. It is time for the warriors, the healers, the shamans, the mystics, the teachers, and the sages to recognize and accept their role in the present moment and recover our connection to the whole.

# Nature Deficit

*The natural world's benefits to our condition and health will be irrelevant if we continue to destroy the nature around us. That destruction is assured without a human reconnection to nature.*
—Richard Louv

These days we are plugged into everything. Handheld mobile wifi platforms are making it possible to stay connected everywhere we go. Wall-sized, flat-screen, high-definition televisions dominate our living spaces, feeding us a never-ending diet of information and advertising. Facebook, Twitter, Snapchat, Instagram, and texting have become the preferred method for keeping in touch with people. We rush around from one thing to the next, spending every spare moment checking our smart phone. There is no doubt that it can be stimulating to feel so connected, and yet there is a feeling of underlying emptiness. We have lost something. The more plugged into technology, the more we are disconnected from the rhythms of nature.

Take a moment to reflect on your daily life and determine how much time you spend in front of the computer, on the phone, watching television, texting, blogging, facebooking, or whatever. Now subtract the amount of time you spend sitting outside, walking in the woods, gardening, or otherwise interacting with nature.

The result is your nature deficit.

The bigger the nature deficit, the more out of balance you are with the life force of the natural world. Being out of balance can affect every part of your life and become a chronic problem.

In his book *Last Child in the Woods* Richard Louv postulated that human beings, especially children, are spending less time outdoors, which results in a wide range of behavioral problems. This is reinforced by sensationalist media coverage that has literally made people scared to be outside exploring the woods, wading in a stream, or wandering across a field. Fearful parents are making their children stay indoors to keep them safe from dangers that have become exaggerated. The hype regarding "stranger danger" and insect-borne disease promotes a culture of fear that encourages regimented sports activities and electronic stimulation over any sort of outdoor imaginative play. Unfortunately, this disrupts the child's ability to connect to nature and the planet as a whole. Being afraid creates a barrier to their learning to love and respect their natural surroundings.

E. O. Wilson, a renowned biologist, believes that we are hard wired with an innate affinity for nature. Philosopher and psychoanalyst Erich Fromm calls this biophilia. However, if children do not have the opportunity to explore and develop that biophilia during their early years, the opposite may take hold. Biophobia is an aversion to nature and can range from a simple phobia of being outside, to contempt for anything that is not man-made, to the attitude that nature is nothing more than a disposable resource to be used, exploited, and discarded as needed. Instilling such a callous disregard for the plants and animals we share this planet with escalates the destruction. And, as the damage to the planet grows, we see a rise in anxiety, depression, and attention-deficit problems. We are creating a catch-22 situation that leads to a dead end. When we lose respect for the planet, we also lose respect for ourselves.

On the other hand, children are happier, healthier, and more creative when they have a connection to nature. This connection has a positive effect on children with attention-deficit problems, asthma, and obesity. Being in nature relieves stress and improves physical health. Adults who work in spaces incorporating nature are more productive, healthy, and creative. Even hospital patients with a view of nature from their window heal faster. How did we forget this connection?

All living things are connected by the life force that flows through them. If you can imagine this connection as billions and billions of tiny web-like fibers linking all things in creation, you can begin to understand how we are intertwined. This web of life is made up of the life-force energy that is part of everything. And every living thing is part of it. The plants and animals of the world, including humans, all have a relationship to one another. At the most basic level this is obvious. It is no accident that the oxygen we breathe is a byproduct of the plants as they go through the life process of photosynthesis, just as the carbon dioxide we exhale is exactly what plants require to live. But the connection goes even deeper than that. In their book *The Secret Life of Plants* Peter Tompkins and Christopher Bird proved, in experiment after experiment, that plants have a much more complex interaction with the world around them than we

8

think they do. Plants react to thoughts, feelings, and emotions as do animals. These reactions could be called "humanlike" if we were to be so arrogant as to assume we are the ones that originally developed such reactions.

Unfortunately, something seems to have gone wrong. We have lost the capacity to *feel* what we are doing to the planet. We have lost our connection to nature as we rush to cut down the forests, mine the mountains, and frack everything else in between. We are destroying the habitats of wild creatures and making much of the world uninhabitable. We don't realize or even seem to care that we are damaging the web of life and, ultimately, ourselves. The reason for this is our nature deficit. When we are disconnected from the natural world, we lose our ability to have empathy for what is going on. Our obsession with technological innovation and our infatuation with electronic connectivity cuts us off from the web of life-force energy and replaces it with an artificial construct, in many ways similar to the concept portrayed in the movie *The Matrix*.

Most people do not realize that when they turn on their television, they are seeing a repetitive pattern of flickering images, which creates a state similar to hypnosis. Studies have shown that within the first minute of television viewing, brain waves switch from predominantly *beta* waves, indicating alert and conscious attention, to predominantly *alpha* waves, indicating an unfocused, receptive lack of attention. Our brain's left hemisphere, the part that processes information logically and analytically, tunes out while the right hemisphere, which processes information emotionally and noncritically, is allowed to function without hindrance. The result is that when viewing television, we do not consciously rationalize the information resonating in our unconscious. We become more open and suggestible to the messages being conveyed.

Is it any wonder that, in a world where children spend an average of forty-four hours a week connected in some way to electronic media, levels of anxiety, depression, and attention-deficit have gone through the roof? And it is no better for adults who have spent their whole lives with television.

It is a difficult proposition, but we need to reconnect with nature to bring our lives back into balance. And, let me be clear, watching a show about nature on the Discovery Channel does not count. If we want to protect our environment and biodiversity, creating opportunities to reconnect with nature is crucial for both children and adults. We need to spend more time unplugged and find ways to let nature balance our lives.

## Unplug

*Remember Now*

*The Time has Come*

*To do Important Things*

*Go Outside*

*Touch the Earth*

*Breathe, and Cry and Sing*

*I Know It's Hard*

*Impossible?*

*A Very Tough Decision*

*Make it Now*

*Turn it Off*

*Unplug your Television*

*—Aaron Hoopes*

# The Heart of Nature

*Walk as if you are kissing the Earth with your feet.*
*—Thich Nhat Hanh*

Recent discoveries in neuroscience have proven that more than 50 percent of the heart is comprised of neural cells. It is from our hearts that we process our energetic connection to everything we come in contact with. The problem is that we have cut ourselves off from this connection by allowing ourselves to be distracted by technology and all of its associated noise. We cannot hear it if we are not listening.

The consciousness of the Earth is vastly different from our individualistic understanding of consciousness. Interacting with the natural world is not simply talking about it or going outside. It is not watching it on the television. It is not eating vegetables from the store. It is much more about opening the lines of communication with nature on an energetic level and sharing our life force. By opening our hearts and experiencing nature in its fullness we begin to realize this connection. It is a purely experiential exercise. We have to spend time in nature to truly feel it. Nature will quiet your mind, open your heart, and invite calm and peace into your body if you allow it to. It enables you to feel the living connection with life around you and gives you the capacity to open up to something much bigger than yourself.

If you are reading this, then it is likely that you already understand what I am saying. You have felt this connection to nature. You have probably also felt the frequency of distraction that comes from electronic technology and the myriad of things that vie for our attention in the busy, hectic world. It is also likely that you know someone who is completely caught up in that frequency and is unplugged from nature. It is time to pass this message on and change the dynamic that has trapped us.

We shape ourselves by the thoughts we hold in our minds. These thoughts create the reality we live in. Holding negative thoughts shapes our world into something we fear. When we are fearful, things we encounter reinforce our negative thoughts. This generates an energy field that surrounds us and encourages unwelcome situations. It is easy to get caught in a downward spiral. Fortunately, the opposite is true as well. If you are generating positive, life-affirming thoughts, things spiral upward as the world becomes a loving and nurturing place.

One of the drawbacks of our highly complex society is that we have become very distracted. There are so many things that vie for our attention that we struggle to discern what is actually relevant and vital to our well-being. These distractions keep us from focusing on some of the important fundamental aspects of life. When the attachment to technological innovations makes us forget the magical world that exists outside in nature or the busyness of daily life fragments our mental process, gaps are created for negative thoughts to take hold.

If we are able to carve out some time to spend in the natural world, we give ourselves an opportunity to bring some balance back into our lives. By acknowledging nature, we learn to sense the vital spirit that exists within all things and this enables us to restore balance and well-being to our lives. Cultivating this connection is essential, yet it is virtually ignored in our supposedly advanced society.

The time has come to transform, awaken, and heal. We can no longer afford to ignore it. We need to begin the process of plugging back into nature, of cultivating our relationship with all living beings, of recognizing the sacredness within. We need to breathe deeply and open ourselves to the life force and energy of the world as a whole.

# Chapter 2
# Deeper Understanding

## Globalized Addiction

*Global society is drowning in addiction to drug use and a thousand other habits. This is because people around the world, rich and poor alike, are being torn from the close ties to family, culture, and traditional spirituality that constituted the normal fabric of life in pre-modern times. This kind of global society subjects people to unrelenting pressures towards individualism and competition, dislocating them from social life. People adapt to this dislocation by concocting the best substitutes that they can for a sustaining social, cultural and spiritual wholeness, and addiction provides this substitute for more and more of us.*
      *—Bruce Alexander*

  In his book *The Globalization of Addiction*, Bruce Alexander observes that the exploitation of the planet for power and profit called the free-market system has torn people away from the close ties to family, culture, and traditional spirituality that constituted the normal fabric of life. This has resulted in dislocating them psychologically and spiritually from the Earth, one another, and themselves. The consequence of such dislocation can be recognized as a type of addiction, the normal human coping response to this type of pressure and objectification.

  Over the last several hundred years, the dominant institutions (governing, political, religious, social/media, commerce) have supported an unsustainable economic system and given way to a new type of society. First the church replaced the warlord, then the state replaced the church; and now we are in a transition through which the transnational corporation is beginning to replace the state. Historically, the social structure and meaning-making aspects of life and communities were independent of the economic system. Meaning and purpose were derived from myths, stories, intergenerational family structure, and sacred traditions. This has shifted so that the economic system of the transnational corporation is the source of structure and meaning for society. But this new kind of meaning lacks a connection to the life of the planet. It is a story based on resource extraction industries and global capitalism without regard for the Earth. The result for the individual is that myth, story, and family lore—the meaning-providing structures for people—get lost in a society based on an economic structure where consumption, greed, and accumulation are given the highest value and those who profess these behaviors are rewarded. As the economic system becomes the dominant source of meaning, direction, and purpose, the historical meaning-making processes fade as each generation is more saturated by commercialization than the one before.

The fracturing and loss of the narratives that once provided meaning, direction, social and personal cohesion, and a sense of purpose result in identity crises for individuals and society. And the anxiety from the identity crisis moves people to cope in different ways. Because this transnational corporate takeover of our lives is all-encompassing and is intensifying, finding healthy ways to resolve this anxiety is becoming more and more difficult. We become dislocated from history (if sports and entertainment is your history, you have no history) and from place; we have nowhere to ground and center ourselves, no space for healing. This dislocation is one of the fundamental causes of globalized addiction.

The expansion of consumer society and unfettered free-market economics to every corner of the globe has had a series of harmful effects on our emotional, spiritual, psychological, and family lives, resulting in a devastating flood of addictions that we've developed in order to cope. We have reached a point where the economic system no longer contributes to the well-being of the planet and society.

Profit has become the primary concern. It fundamentally changes what we think of as normal. If we live in a world where profit has more meaning than family or community, where competition is essential for survival, where we seem powerless to make even small changes in our lives, we begin to feel insecure, isolated, and fearful. The hyper-free-market economic system most of us live immersed in is by definition competitive and profit based (capital must grow or the system collapses), and each participant is defined by her or his success at accumulating more and more. When catastrophic oil spills, war, poverty, pollution, anxiety, and depression and the practices that produced these patterns become normalized, addiction is a natural and reasonable human response.

We actually need some form of recovery process to break us out of this addictive cycle, to reinvigorate the human spirit so that we can sense that we are part of the spirituality of this planet. We need to feel our connection to being a participant of this great and wonderful living being we call Earth. When we join with others in this recovery process, we will garner the strength to intervene in the addictive behaviors that are destroying the planet. We can form groups and create spaces where we can speak gently but speak the truth, and provide comfort for the despair that will come when people wake up and face for the first time the realization that the planet is moving toward lifelessness. In small community groups, people can explore their vision of loving this Earth and loving life and doing what it takes to ensure that we continue into the future. When we do this, the younger generations can begin to hear an alternative to what they have been told and hopefully start to realize that there might be a different way.

# Distorting Reality

*Addiction is any process over which we are powerless. It takes control of us, causing us to do and think things that are inconsistent with our personal values and leading us to become progressively more compulsive and obsessive. A sure sign of an addiction is the sudden need to deceive ourselves and others—to lie, deny, and cover up.*

—Anne Wilson Schaef

We know in our bones and in our souls that for life to have meaning, we must be more than a cog in an economic wheel. Many people feel deeply that something is wrong. As we become conscious that something is indeed wrong, our first response is often to think something is wrong with ourselves. We feel guilty, inadequate, shameful, possibly helpless to change what is wrong, and the normal human response to feeling like that is to find something to make it stop. Most often we adopt behaviors that may involve drugs, alcohol, shopping, work, food, sex, gambling, self-absorption, ideology, television, video games, and more; you can add to the list any number of activities. When we adopt one of these behaviors and use it to feel okay about ourselves, it is an addiction. Usually the addiction is something that continues the cycle of guilt and shame and helplessness, even as it soothes our sense of disconnection and papers over the pain.

What does this look like? An addiction to work and to wasteful consumption can provide a sense of success, status, and membership in our free-market society. But it cannot meet the human need for real connection and belonging. So we work harder and buy more, which still cannot meet our true needs, and, when multiplied millions of times over, leads to the destruction of our true home, Earth. The sense that something is wrong grows stronger, and we work more feverishly to acquire more money and more stuff to try and feel complete. And so the cycle goes on.

Of course, whenever the subject of addiction is addressed, the distorting of reality emerges as a core issue that needs to be dealt with. The addict must maintain a grip on denial in order to avoid direct conversation and confrontation. The addict fights anything that might impact their lifestyle and behavior. And while addiction for the individual can be self-destructive, an addictive distraction of a whole nation is often much deadlier. In hindsight, one could conclude that the Vietnam and Iraq wars were a distraction while power was being consolidated in the military-industrial complex of the United States. Another example is the world of media entertainment, including the "news" channels, which are really a front for corporate interests that do not get challenged in the public space and often simply parrot the press releases of the government. These distractions can be creative, intense, playful, deceitful, and deadly.

It can also be very difficult to break the pattern of denial. Most of us are familiar with statements like: "I don't have a drinking problem." "I just had one cookie." "The radiation (or mercury, or lead, or fluoride, or whatever) levels are safe." "Fracking is not harmful to the water supply." "I only watch the Discovery Channel." Denial is certainly not just a river in Egypt.

We often try to convince ourselves of things we know are not true because to admit otherwise would throw a spotlight on the facade of our lives and society, and threaten to collapse our carefully created world. So instead, we go deeper into the addiction. We consume more and more while telling ourselves everything is fine.

The physical toll of addiction, whether of an individual, family, or nation, ranges from premature death to a zombie-type existence. The cost to the family ranges from stress and depression to divorce to developing a relational coping system that has been called co-dependency. The social toll is the loss of a person's potential to participate fully in life and the life of the community. The financial cost to the nation can be incredible: according to the National Institute on Drug Abuse, the annual cost of substance abuse (illegal drugs, pharmaceuticals, alcohol, and tobacco) to the US economy was $700 billion in 2015. How can we comprehend the amount of denial and reality distortion needed to maintain a 700-billion-dollar habit a year in the US alone? And these are only statistics for substances that we've collectively agreed to call addictive. Add to that the cost of addictions to food, sex, mass media, information technology, consumerism, and violence and we have the makings of a problem of monstrous proportions.

# Freedom Relinquished

*Once the primary bonds which gave security to the individual are severed, once the individual faces the world outside himself as a completely separate entity, two courses are open to him. One is moving through the anxiety toward a positive freedom characterized by spontaneity, creativity, and living life with a sense of fulfillment. This is life where dreams can be actualized for the dreams are connected to real possibilities. The other is a person can fall back and give up freedom.*

—*Erich Fromm*

Contemporary society encourages self-awareness only within a narrow, controlled framework through standardized education, mass media, and a false us-vs-them paradigm. At the same time, it tears people away from their union with nature and others. This combination of lack of connection with nature and others and having self-awareness contributes to feelings of loneliness, isolation, and homelessness. Life becomes characterized by addictions, dreams that are not possible, unhappy relationships, a lack of empathy and compassion. All of this breeds anxiety. Human beings then defend this resulting anxiety by turning to a way of life characterized by three detrimental aspects.

# Authoritarianism

Authoritarianism is an uncompromising allegiance to a group, ideology, political party, theology, or nation. The authoritarian personality formation needs an opposing object, a person, group, idea, or scapegoat. This sense of superiority allows for the tolerance of the suffering of others. In effect, it creates a system of denial counter to a reality-based understanding of life.

The predominant political climate of developed nations and the leading transnational corporations have resulted in an authoritarian movement composed of those with a psychological and emotional need to follow a strong authority figure who provides them with a sense of a perceived moral clarity and a feeling of individual power. By definition, its followers' devotion to authority and the movement's own power is supreme, thereby overriding the consciences of its individual members and removing any intellectual and moral limits on what will be justified in defense of their movement.

Authoritarianism is a response to being torn from nature. The sense of dislocation caused by the lack of a deep connection to the Earth can often manifest itself in this manner, either becoming the authority or the follower in the authoritative expression. When the primary bonds from our source of life are broken, the human will seek secondary bonds as a way to compensate. When the young child draws strength from the parent figure (primary bond), the child borrows from the caregiver's ego until they are able to solidify their own sense of self. When that primary bond is not available, anxiety will result and the child will seek connection to an external source to comfort the anxiety. The secondary source could be another trusting adult, resulting in a positive compensatory outcome. Unfortunately, it is often something less positive such as television, food, or fighting with a sibling.

In adulthood, when the subconscious experiences the loss of the connection to nature, the secondary source of comfort can be any number of things: a person, a religious figure, a political figure, the bully at school, the idolized celebrity, a sports team, or a belief system. This comfort then forms a process of understanding reality that can become a filter of all experiences, and everything and everyone is judged through that filter.

Aggressive authoritarianism has three distinct tendencies: (1) the need to make others dependent and to have absolute power over them; (2) to exploit others, to use them, commodify them, to steal from them (including natural resources from other nations), to rob others of their life physically, intellectually, spiritually, and emotionally, to manipulate people to live as you see fit, structure their lives so they buy from the company store and create a society where the cost of living is just a bit more than you pay them; and (3) to create suffering and enjoy suffering, to humiliate, and to embarrass.

## Conformity

Conformity is a process of self-protection when someone has no other way of coping with the anxiety and sense of isolation that is prevalent in our world today. People will merge into the sameness of society when feeling overwhelmed and their problems appear bigger than they can deal with. As a result, a person is vulnerable to change one's ideal self to conform to a perception of society's, losing one's true self in the process. When the outside world becomes overwhelming, the inner world fragments and an inner cohesion that characterizes spiritual health is lost.

When the reality of the world is too much and stimulation is more than the child or the adult can assimilate and make meaning of, a psychological defense will emerge and short circuit the deliberative mental process of meaning-making. It is at this time that we are most vulnerable to shift to conformity. Conformity offers comfort and a reduction of anxiety or at least a sharing of the anxiety. Unfortunately, it does resolve the anxiety and the defenses need to be kept in place. Coercion intensifies toward conformity to a society that serves a particular economic power structure and consequently demands that individuals tow the line. We become a society of false selves. Is it any wonder that modern media, with the many movies, TV shows, and books on the living dead and the zombie apocalypse are so popular? Art is providing a mirror for us to observe ourselves.

Conformity is a difficult confession for any individual to make. No one is going to say "I am conformed to consumerism and I am proud of it. So dedicated am I, I have organized my life to support the buying of items I really do not need and will soon throw out and gladly participate in the destruction of the Earth." We all have the belief that we are as unique as fingerprints or snowflakes. We also understand how feelings and thoughts can be induced from the outside and yet be subjectively experienced as one's own, and how one's own feelings and thoughts can be repressed and thus cease to be part of daily life. But most of us convince ourselves that we are immune to the effects or that we are too smart to be influenced by it. Yet, how often do we parrot what we have heard on TV or read on a website as our own thought?

## Destruction

Destructiveness is different from authoritarianism and conformity since it aims not at active or passive symbiosis but at elimination of its object. The person possessed by this tendency will organize life in such a way his or her very identity merges with the intended target of destruction. The imagination is filled with the life of the one that must be destroyed. The obsession will result in the person or groups structuring their lives to eliminate the other. Examples of this can be found in those who join or align themselves with hate groups, religious extremism, or even patriotism. This attitude is most often expressed against those perceived as being in power. If by some chance the target is eliminated, another will soon be found.

The tendency of the destructive defense against isolation and the sense of powerlessness functions as a human-bonding and community-building device, albeit an expression of negative bonding. For this group, there is no greater celebration than to collectively organize their lives to destroy someone, an idea, or another group. The destruction process leads to a frenzy and with that energy and success the next target is selected and on it goes. It is the process of destruction that is important rather than the object. The merger with others in this destructive process is the closest one can get to genuine intimacy and love. This is why the allegiance is so intense and formidable.

The intensity of the destructiveness, and the extent to which one organizes one's life toward the destruction of the other person, group, idea, or the Earth, is in proportion to the extent that the inner life has been thwarted. The person lives with a diminished capacity never realizing the potential of life: sensuality, emotional experience, curiosity, relationships, and intellectual life. As the inner life becomes more lifeless, the protest against the destruction of the external world grows hauntingly silent.

None of these three responses is going to be of any positive help to the individual. In fact, authoritarianism, conformity, and destruction will only increase the pain and suffering for everyone on the planet . . . including the planet itself.

# Changing the Narrative

## Blessed Be the Earth

*Blessed be the Earth that forms at last*

*The remnants of supernovas brilliant show in deep space,*
*Over the eons swirling helium, hydrogen, giving birth to stars and*
*planets.*

*Our home our mother earth pulling herself together, tighter and*
*tighter fire and water, rock and sea, land and air, storm and calm,*
*plant and animal, tree and human.*

*From the soil and water we emerged from the air we breathe and in*
*the air we walk.*

*We are in this Earth*

*We are on this Earth*

*We are sustained by this Earth*

*We are fed by this Earth*

*We are of this Earth*

*Blessings upon this living being of which we are a part.*

*—Gregory Wilson*

Used with permission, © Gregory Wilson

A narrative or story is the telling of connected events in a sequence of written or spoken words. It derives from the Latin verb *narrare*, "to tell." The narrative that we live in defines the boundaries of what we believe is our reality. There are any number of narratives governing our lives at any given time. The duties, obligations, and behaviors of a father, mother, son, daughter, student, teacher, employee, consumer are all different yet there is a larger narrative going on as well . . . as human beings on the planet. That narrative has been written by the religions, societies, and civilizations that came before us. It has evolved over time until we reach the narrative of our present society, which is the trouble we find ourselves in now. It is a narrative based on fossil fuels, globalization, big business, banking, politics, and conflict. The technological advances of the present day are getting better and better at reinforcing that narrative within us on a daily basis. It is used to explain and justify the status quo. It distracts us from what is truly important. It tells us we are individuals, each with our own wants and needs that are more important than the whole.

That narrative divides us. It creates fear that helps to keep us disconnected from one another and the Earth as a whole. The old story, the one in which we are now living, was/is characterized by the mythological themes of progress and manifest destiny. The outcome of living this story and intensifying the cultural supports, generation after generation, is the maturing of the themes of authoritarianism, conformity, and destructiveness. However, this story of human culture was/is taking place in a much larger story: the story of the universe and the story of the Earth.

The time has come to change the narrative. We need to start telling ourselves a different story. One that is inclusive of not only all the people of the planet, but also the plants, animals, insects, and every other living being.

# The Story of Earth

*We are about the Great Work. We all have our particular work—some of us are teachers, some of us are healers, some of us in various professions, some of us are farming. We have a variety of occupations. But beside the particular work we do and the particular lives we lead, we have a Great Work that everyone is involved in and no one is exempt from. That is the work of moving on from a terminal Cenozoic Era to an emerging Ecozoic Era in the story of the planet Earth . . . which is the Great Work.*
—*Thomas Berry*

In the Earth story, the present chapter is called the Cenozoic era. It is 65 million pages, each page being a year long, and during this chapter of Earth's story, life simply flourished. Think of your most idyllic image and experience of nature—a one-hundred-foot waterfall with a pool at the bottom where you can swim, diving under water and being surrounding by the sea life, sitting on a rock outcrop looking up and seeing a hawk circling and climbing higher and higher, kayaking with dolphins, sitting on your porch and watching bees moving from flower to flower, standing in stillness in the woods and just listening, waking up to the song of birds, hearing the call of an owl in the night, the wind through the trees drawing you to a walk in the woods, standing in a field of wildflowers and sharing with your child . . . just pause for a moment and the result of 65 million years of life producing life will come to you and nature will capture your spirit and life will be celebrated in your imagination. The wonder and life of your imagination is an outcome of the flourishing of life during the Cenozoic era. Life was simply everywhere. The ending of this chapter in the story of Earth has been, and is being written, by humans. The life-producing theme at the heart of the Cenozoic chapter is now giving way to the theme of the diminishing of Earth's life-supporting systems. This theme in Earth's story began with the industrial revolution. Today, 21 billion pounds of toxic chemicals are released each year into the environment; of these over 2 million tons (over 4.5 billion pounds) per year are recognized carcinogens. We have entered a stage in Earth's history where natural selection is giving way to cultural selection. The normal unfolding of the Earth will not determine the future of the planet. Instead, whatever human culture is dominant will determine that future. The out-of-sync rhythm between the life-producing ongoing processes of the Earth and the economic growth process of our present dominant culture cannot coexist. The reason for this is that our present economic growth process requires the extinguishing of the Earth's life-supporting systems.

At this moment, we are between stories. The next chapter in Earth's story needs to be written as an interconnected human-Earth relationship that has not existed previously. If we continue with the old story, including the intensification of the plot themes of authoritarianism, conformity, and destructiveness, the story will end in tragedy. However, we as a people, as interrelated beings on this living planet full of wonder, now have the opportunity of choosing to move in another direction. The concept of relationship needs to be a central theme of this new way of being.

*Mitakuye Oyasin* is a Lakota Sioux term literally translated as "All My Relations." The meaning, however, extends beyond that of the English translation to include not only the human family, but all of the animal, plant, and mineral kingdoms as well as the forces of nature (wind, thunder, lightning, etc.) plus the elements. *Mitakuye Oyasin* is said when greeting nature. It is an opening of the heart and communing directly with the life force of all living beings. It is a recognition of our place within the whole. We are all connected in the intricate web of existence, and each of us is affected by the actions of any other. *Mitakuye Oyasin* is a recognition of our place within the whole. Everything is interrelated; nothing exists in isolation.

This understanding sheds light on the true structure of the universe. It cannot be overstated; we humans are part of the interconnected whole. Thomas Berry has called this new chapter the Ecozoic era. "Ecozoic" means "house of life," an "Ecozoic society" means a society of life. The Ecozoic era is a time of mutually enhancing relationships among humans and the larger community of life.

The ending of the Cenozoic era is a result of two primary conditions. The first is the inner state of the human, the Procrustean condition of our spiritual life. The second is the chemical discharge and waste from the extractive industry centerpiece of the industrial revolution and our present economic system.

By now we understand that living in a cultural context in which the economic and legal structures are human centered results in authoritarianism, conformity to the collective whole, and destructive tendencies becoming substrates of society. The effect on humans is to become psychologically and spiritually dislocated. To move in the direction of gaining the capacity to begin to live and write the introduction to the Ecozoic era, we must have some kind of recovery pathway, a direction. We need to move in the direction of forming and transforming into a culture that is connected to the rhythm-of-life generating systems of the Earth.

A recovery process that includes self-discovery is not just the story of our personal life but also the story of the Earth's life as well as our culture's life and its evolution. It is a process that begins with the acknowledgment that in some manner we have been torn or separated from nature. And this separation is the primary source for the dis-ease and destructive path our society is on. Once we can finally acknowledge this, we can begin the process of healing.

# The New Story

*You cannot teach a man anything;*
*You can only help him find it within himself.*
                                        *—Galileo*

Thomas Berry developed a new conceptual framework based upon what we might call a dynamic and functional cosmological ecology—an ecology (from the Greek "oikos" meaning "household") because it is concerned with the inter-relationships of all species and components within an integrated "Earth household." It is cosmological because it links the origins of the Earth and its species to the origins of the universe. It is dynamic because it stresses both physical and psychic dimensions of a continually developing universe and planet. And it is functional because it is designed to guide our actions into the future. He has called this new conceptual framework "The New Story." And while it is difficult to fully tell this new story—because it is still evolving—certain themes are emerging that seem to form part of the plot line.

# New Story Themes

## The Earth

The Earth is a single integral community composed of multiple and diverse components of being. All the living components of Earth connect to form a mutually enhancing web of life. Our present society has conditioned us to think of the Earth as a collection of separate objects, but there is no separation. The Earth is a communion of beings all living on this planet. This community is a balanced ecosystem that provides the energy and environment to support all the various components. It has the capacity for self-propagation, self-nourishment, self-education, self-governance, self-healing, self-fulfillment, and unfortunately self-destruction. When in balance, this community cares for and nourishes all of its components.

## The Nature of Development

As a living organism, the Earth and each of its components develop in the manner of all other organisms. They have certain inherent developmental tendencies. They go through similar stages of life. They can differentiate themselves from other species. They can assume their own distinct identity and attain consciousness. The components have the ability to self-organize. Conscious components have the capacity to enter into communion with the Earth and all its other components. There is an intimate relationship with all living things on the planet, both animate and inanimate. Each component develops at its own pace and rhythm.

## The Human Species

The hardest thing to understand concerning human nature and destiny as a species is to grasp the reality that we are a species in a relationship with the whole integrated Earth community. Each one of us is a part of the whole. If humans understand this life principle and their connection to the Earth, the Earth and its well-being should become a primary concern. Human well-being is derived from the well-being of the Earth. A healthy planet provides a healthy environment for the beings living on it. The healthy beings nurture the planet.

## The Present Situation

As stated earlier, we now find ourselves in a dire situation confronting a massive set of challenges. The human species, along with the rest of the integrated Earth community, is at a critical point of our development. The Earth, in its present mode of existence, is being devastated as the planet's life-support systems—water, air, atmosphere, topsoil, forests, oceans—are being used up, are being contaminated, or are dying. Species are disappearing at an unprecedented rate. The main factor for this is the drive to develop national and world economies at the expense of the Earth community. Very few are able to recognize that all economic development is dependent upon and constrained by the development of Earth itself—which is finite. Unlike previous devastations of our planet, which were natural, the present devastation is man-made. The Earth will go on, of that there is no doubt. However, if humans don't rebalance the environmental destruction that we are causing, the Earth will go on without us.

# The Great Work

Berry believed human consciousness is the universe reflecting upon itself. This reflective capacity confers upon us certain ethical and moral responsibilities to care for the planet and the integrated Earth community. The core concept of Berry's Great Work is to recognize, accept, and respect the fundamental laws of nature and Earth jurisprudence, which is a philosophy of law and human governance that is based on the idea that humans are only one part of a wider community of beings and that the welfare of each member of that community is dependent on the welfare of the Earth as a whole.

Our challenge as a human species is to recognize the present situation and take steps to stop the damage, heal the planet, and ensure its future survival and development and ours along with it. Humans and the Earth will go into the future as an integrated Earth community, or we will become extinct. It is a pretty straightforward situation. And while the situation is dire, it is not hopeless, as long as we begin taking steps to reverse things.

As we move into the future, our main focus must be on carrying out the transition from a period of human devastation of the Earth to a period of mutually beneficial coexistence. The Earth was here long before we were and will be here long after our bones have turned to dust. It is not the survival of the Earth that is the issue. It is the human race that is threatened. And it is now time to face our responsibility to implement a practice that brings us in tune with the Earth. The only way to accomplish that is to focus on ourselves.

# Chapter 3
# Rebalancing and Reconnecting

## Staying Present

*First, I need to work to discover my own addictions, and be in some form of recovery.*
—*Chellis Glendinning*

There is an old Chinese proverb that states if you want to correct the world, correct the state; if you want to correct the state, correct the family; if you want to correct the family, correct yourself.

It is time to correct ourselves. There is really no other way we are going to make it through what is to come. We can no longer live in distraction and fear. We must now turn toward what is good and right and just. This means taking responsibility for ourselves and owning what is ours. It means we must start working on being present in every moment of every day, maintaining balance along our path, and reconnecting with the Earth.

Staying present can be a challenge for yogis who live in the mountains and meditate every day. For the rest of us in today's crazy world, it borders on the impossible. But we must now do the impossible if we want to avoid the inevitable. Yes, I understand that there is too much going on in your life, and it often feels like you are one inch from the edge; however, if you are to continue on this journey to connect with the Earth and bring peace, love, and light into the world, staying present is vital. Staying present provides a solid ground from which to focus on difficulties as they arise. It is a way to take control of things and get your life in order. It is no longer an option to spend your time distracting yourself as you try to escape from being present.

Staying present is all the more difficult if we are unaware of how we distract ourselves. There are four ways to distract ourselves from staying present: looking forward, looking backward, looking sideways, and looking away. Each of them presents challenges to overcome, but with an understanding and willingness to do the work we can get to a better place.

# Looking Forward

Looking forward is focusing on the future. This happens when we become diverted from the present moment by wanting things we don't have or wishing for our situation to be different. It also happens when we seek to protect ourselves from the imagined consequences of the present situation we find ourselves in. Another manifestation of looking forward is when we find ourselves in a predicament and spend our time trying to find ways to undo what we have done.

In reality, looking forward is merely an attempt to escape from a present moment we are unhappy with. It is a way of pushing things aside and focusing on something yet to come. However, if we are looking at the goal rather than the needs of the present moment, it is very likely we will stumble over something in the path. The truth is that the only way around a problem is through it. We must learn to face our difficulties with courage and honesty. The creative power of the universe is available if we are able to acknowledge the power of right and good and focus on what is directly in front of us. The chances are that if we are focused on the present moment the situation can be dealt with effectively.

There is nothing necessarily wrong with making plans for the future or considering the consequences of our actions or behaviors. In fact, these can be helpful practices if we are grounded in the present moment. However, when looking forward is used to avoid looking at what we are doing in our lives right now we sabotage the whole process.

# Looking Backward

Looking backward is focusing on the past. This happens when we spend our time wishing we had made different choices about our life. It also happens when we begin blaming ourselves for things that have happened that we regret. We also are looking backward when we feed our ego by congratulating ourselves on things we have accomplished.

Looking backward is simply another method for escaping from the present moment. Unfortunately, all of the longing to turn back time is only going to dig us into a deeper hole. Sometimes it can feel as if we are dragging a whole trail of mistakes, bad choices, and missed opportunities along behind us. It is time to let go of all of that baggage we are carrying. If we are dragging all of that stuff behind us it is impossible to open ourselves to new opportunities and experiences that appear before us. In addition, if we are looking back at where we came from rather than the path forward, we are likely to run smack into something.

The things we've done, the people we've met, the experiences we've had, have all brought us to this present moment. They have made us who we are. We cannot go back and change things. We need to accept where we are no matter the situation and move forward in a positive manner.

*Your life is made up of the choices you make.*
*Every single choice you've made*
*has resulted in exactly where you are right now.*
*Look at your life . . . and it will reveal your thoughts.*
*Your life today is an outcome*
*of where your thoughts have been yesterday,*
*and today is no different.*
*The thoughts you make now*
*are going to create a specific outcome in your life.*
*If you don't leave your past in the past.*
*It will destroy your future.*
*To be happy you must*
*Let go of what is gone,*
*Be grateful for what remains, and*
*Count the simple blessings in life.*
*Live for what today has to offer,*
*not for what yesterday has taken away.*
*Don't stress about the future, it hasn't arrived.*
*Whilst you can be optimistic about what is coming next,*
*Live in the present and make it truthful.*
*—Shanti Gowans*

Used with permission, © Shanti Gowans

# Looking Sideways

Looking sideways is focusing on what others are doing in relation to ourselves. This happens when we spend our time comparing or contrasting our situation with others. It can be a wanting or yearning for something someone else has. We are looking sideways when we are gauging our rate of progress in comparison with the rate of progress of others. It is when we see others with more money, or in a better life situation, and we covet what they have.

Looking sideways is another way of escaping from the present moment. When we try to measure some aspect of ourselves against another it is very easy to get caught up in envy and resentment. Envy comes from the perception that others have more than we do, and resentment comes from the perception that others have it easier. The truth is that everyone is on his or her own journey. Each of us has our own struggles. Someone's good fortune is not to be looked upon with covetous eyes. We must turn our attention away from what other people do or have. If we are looking around at the other people rather than paying attention to our own life, we will get lost. We must learn to focus on ourselves here and now.

# Looking Away

Looking away is looking at just about anything else but ourselves in the present moment. This is when we use all manner of distraction to keep us from dealing with the present situation we find ourselves in. We are looking away when we spend hours on social media with no real purpose, or when we mindlessly watch movies or shows when we could be doing more productive things. It is when we concoct all sorts of reasons and excuses for not doing what we should be doing.

Looking away is very easy. The culture we live in provides so many various options to distract us. Technology and the Internet have made it possible to access information on anything with the touch of a button. With so much information available on every subject it is easy to get lost for hours without even realizing it. The more distracted we get, the more fragmented our attention becomes, which makes it harder to concentrate and easier to get distracted even more.

When we are not satisfied with our lot in life it is very easy to get drawn down into a negative spiral of fear and disappointment. Focusing on looking forward, looking backward, looking sideways, or looking away is a diversion from dealing with the present moment. When we are wishing or wanting a different situation, we are unable to clearly see the situation we are in. When we are blaming others or resenting what they have, we cannot assess our own behavior. When we are distracted and unfocused, we are unable to act spontaneously as the moment demands.

The time has now come for us to pay attention to ourselves. We must begin to give ourselves the opportunity to make positive things happen in our lives. This is a process of allowing ourselves to be guided by the present moment. It starts with learning to pay attention to only that which is right here before us. As we begin to cultivate an attitude that is concerned with what is happening right now in front of us we begin to realize what it is that we need to do to move forward in a positive manner. We are able to discern what is essential and correct and can move in that direction.

## Rebalancing Practice

*The major work of the world is not done by geniuses. It is done by ordinary people, with balance in their lives, who have learned to work in an extraordinary manner.*
*—Gordon B. Hinkley*

Rebalancing ourselves and our lives can mean many things. It means paying attention to our inner worlds (how we are breathing, whether calm or in turmoil, feelings of contentment or anxiety, undercurrents of security or fearfulness) and our outer worlds (family, neighborhood, society, work-world, nature). It is time for us to recognize and fully understand that when we are in balance, things move smoothly. This is the essence of *reconnecting to the Earth*. If we are vibrating on the same wavelength as the world then everything around us is as it should be. When we achieve that kind of balance, we start to truly know who we are as individuals, and how we connect with the larger world around us. Being in balance helps to give us a sense of freedom, security, safety, and belonging. For most of us it is not always easy, however, to remain in balance when it feels like the whole world around us is careening out of control. Indeed, once we find ourselves out of balance it can take a lot of effort to get it back. When we are out of balance, it is imperative that conscious, focused steps be taken to get ourselves back in balance.

When undertaking a rebalancing it is important to start with things that will support and guide us as we move further into the process of reconnecting with the whole. This is when we truly start to rediscover our connection to the Earth. It is a life-altering process that we may find to be quite challenging but totally worth it in the long run.

# Rebalancing the Body

When beginning any life-changing practice it is important to start with something that will jump-start the process and motivate us to continue. It needs to be something that can assist with the more difficult aspects of the endeavor. It needs to start with our body. The body is our physical presence in the world. It is the vessel with which we navigate the outside world. It is also the part of us that we have the most personal control over. If the body is unhealthy, underdeveloped, or damaged, it will be much more difficult to deal with the challenges that life places before us. It is also highly unrealistic that we will have the energy or ability to focus our attention on any of the more complex and deeper aspects of ourselves if our body is not a worthy ally in the endeavor. Our body is the vessel we will need to navigate these changes. It must be ready for the challenge. It must be working properly. The only way to reclaim our connection to nature and the Earth is to start a process that brings us into alignment with that energy. It must start in the body. The body is the part of our being we have the most control over. We need to begin with a practice that is going to get our body feeling better and energize it at the same time. Therefore, the absolute first thing we must get working properly is our breathing.

# Breathwork

Deep-breathing practice, often called breathwork, is the first and most important practice of rebalancing the body. Breathing is one of the fundamental aspects of our physical selves. It is something we do all day, every day, in a continuous rhythm throughout our lives from the moment we are born to the day we die. Unfortunately for many, breathing is a very shallow and unconscious process that merely brings in enough oxygen to keep the body functioning at a basic survival level. Like a subsistence farmer who scrapes away on a dusty piece of land to grow barely enough food to feed himself, this type of breathing does nothing to assist us in doing anything more than staying alive. This unconscious, subsistence breathing can keep the body functioning by maintaining the basic systems of the body for many years. However, it does not provide energy for much of anything else.

Breathing is fundamental to human existence. The human body can survive without food for days or even weeks. It can survive without water perhaps for a couple of days. However, without oxygen, we die in minutes. It is quite incongruous that most people spend a great part of their lives concerned with their eating and drinking habits yet, for the most part, pay very little attention to their breathing. It would be like fixing up a car, polishing the chrome, tuning the engine, inflating the tires, and then not filling it with gasoline. We won't get very far that way.

Learning to breathe correctly and effectively is the first step in rebalancing ourselves and maintaining the health of the body. Even with just a basic understanding of the circulatory system, it makes perfect sense. We take in oxygen from the air we breathe. The oxygen enters our bloodstream and creates the oxygen-rich blood that flows through our veins. The blood liberates the energy in the food we ingest. At the same time, it collects the toxins and poisons generated through our everyday living and expels them as $CO_2$. When our breathing is unconscious and shallow, this process is not working up to its potential, and all sorts of disease and problems are much more likely to take hold. It also stands to reason that if we learn to breathe deeper and take in more oxygen, that would give us more energy-producing oxygen-rich blood to flow through our veins. In addition, the expansion of lung capacity would enable us to expel more toxins and poisons. It is as if deep breathing turbo charges the whole process.

By learning simple deep-breathing exercises the body becomes infused with more oxygen and vital energy. Practicing deep breathing whenever there is a free moment or opportunity allows a fundamental shift to take place. The body begins to feel better. As the body feels better, we start to breathe easier and fuller, which in turn brings in even more oxygen and energy. The simple action of noticing the breath brings our awareness to it and increases its quality. As we become more adept at being conscious of our breathing during our daily lives, we create opportunities to notice the magic of the world around us. Breathing in this manner slows us down and roots us in the present moment. It is a simple, yet profound first step on this path . . . and we have to start somewhere.

# Exercise 1

## *The Complete Breath*

The Complete Breath is a dynamic deep-breathing exercise that is both simple and beneficial. Regular practice cleans and invigorates the lungs while expanding lung capacity. Expanded lung capacity naturally slows down our unconscious breathing process, making it smoother and more regular. In addition, the complete breath maximizes oxygen intake and causes oxygen-rich blood to flow more readily to the extremities. As we practice, we should start to feel an overall warmth pervading the body as our blood and energy begins to circulate better.

In the beginning, it is best if the complete breath is practiced from a lying-down posture so maximum concentration can be placed on the exercise itself. Lying down takes all of the attention away from trying to support the body and encourages deep relaxation. Once you become comfortable with the process, you can try different positions such as sitting or standing. Eventually you want to get to the point where you can practice it anywhere at any time.

The exercise consists of four separate steps: inhalation, retention, exhalation, suspension.

### Inhalation

Calmly and peacefully inhale through the nose. Expand your lower abdomen, pushing out and down, as if you are drawing the breath deep into your belly. Once your abdomen is full, continue inhaling and expand your chest from the bottom up. Then fill your upper lungs. Raise your collarbone and shoulders as you continue inhaling. Remember, this is a muscular action in addition to being a respiratory action. Using the muscles of the abdomen to push out and down creates a vacuum that allows the lungs to expand to their full capacity. Feel your whole body filling up so that finally your throat and nose are full. Stop.

## Retention

In a relaxed and non-stressful manner, hold your breath in. Feel as if this is simply a pause that allows you to become aware of your body and let everything settle down. Gradually bring your attention to the fullness of your body. Feel the sensations as the oxygen-rich blood circulates throughout your body. Notice any particular feelings within. Become aware of any aches and pains without allowing them to take over your attention. Remain calm and relaxed. Continue to hold the breath in for a count of ten. Shorten the hold time if it feels uncomfortable.

## Exhalation

When you are ready, slowly begin to exhale. You can exhale through either your nose or your mouth. Exhaling through your mouth is more energizing, while exhaling through your nose is more meditative and relaxed. Practice one way for a while and then try the other. As you are breathing out, begin to contract your lower abdomen by compressing it inward and upward. Continue to exhale by squeezing the air from your lungs and chest. Push it out gently, don't overstrain. Gently lower your collarbones and shoulders, and then blow the air from your throat and nose. Empty it all out. Stop.

## Suspension

Again, in a gentle, relaxed manner, hold your breath out. This is another pause to bring you fully into your body. Allow your attention to focus on the emptiness of your body. Notice any particular feelings within. Become aware of any aches and pains but do not allow them to take over your attention. Remain calm and relaxed. Feel as if your body is an empty balloon waiting to be filled. Continue to suspend breathing for a count of ten. Shorten the time if it feels uncomfortable.

**Repeat**

On the next inhalation don't gasp for air. Calmly and smoothly inhale just as before, deep, long, and slow. Feel the air reaching far beyond your abdomen, filling every corner of your body like an expanding balloon. Notice the sensation of your body as the new oxygen is brought in.

Practice the whole exercise for at least five breaths. Gradually try to increase the number of breaths as you become more adept at the exercise. Eventually you want to be able to do a complete breath anywhere, at any time throughout the day. Then do it.

# Movement

Breathing is not the only thing fundamental to life. Without movement, things begin to grow stagnant and stiffen. Movement is the process of applying the benefits of breathing to the body. Using breathwork to draw in sufficient oxygen to charge the blood is the first step; however, we need to be able to move that energized blood to all the various parts of the body that need it. For this to happen, circulation is the key. The heart pumps oxygen- and nutrient-rich blood into the arteries, which deliver it to the cells and tissues. In addition, it also flushes out the old or stagnated blood and removes impurities that have accumulated in the body. The smooth circulation of the blood provides energy and cleanses the body, allowing the internal organs to function without excessive strain. It also bolsters our immune system so we are less vulnerable to disease.

While breathing is the key to bringing energy into the body, physical movement is needed to process and direct the energy effectively. Critical to the body's proper functioning, movement assures that the vital flow continues once the energy is absorbed. Without movement, circulation is constricted and blood cannot flow freely and smoothly. As blood flow decreases, the amount of oxygen that reaches the extremities is reduced. Stagnation occurs in these areas, and they become vulnerable to injury and disease or, if already injured, they do not heal properly. The heart then starts to pump harder to compensate for lack of circulation and the lungs begin to gasp for air. But, since the body has not been conditioned by movement to assure the ample intake and circulation of oxygen, the stress and strain on the heart and lungs can, at best, be draining. With movement, the heart provides the force that drives circulation by pumping blood through the body. Movement raises the heart rate, increasing the ability of the heart to pump blood effectively. Proper distribution of blood and energy assist the organic and musculoskeletal systems to maintain themselves. In this way, all the bodily systems are kept active and healthy.

In the practice of rebalancing we go back to what the human body was designed for—physical labor. Sadly, in our present sedentary society, the body's natural need for and impulse toward movement are inhibited. School, job, and other interests often keep us sitting still for much of the day. We drive short distances in our cars and spend our free time in front of the TV or computer screen. Modern science and technology have undermined our natural propensity for movement through the introduction of a vast array of labor-saving devices, pharmaceutical drugs, and medical procedures that help us to actually survive for a time in a sedentary lifestyle. If we can begin to remember how essential movement is to human health, we can then start consciously making physical activity a cornerstone of our natural and healthy life.

When we recognize that the body needs movement to be healthy, it creates an opportunity to do something about it. We know that when we're hungry we should eat, and when we're tired we should sleep. But when our muscles get stiff or achy and our body feels sluggish, we are likely to ignore or misinterpret what the body is telling us—that we need to move, to engage in something that gets the heart pumping, the muscles limbered up, and the blood flowing. In fact, our inclination often is to think just the opposite, that we need rest rather than exercise.

If you have a rechargeable battery that is out of energy you don't recharge it by setting it on the couch and letting it watch TV. No, you zap it with electrical current to refill its depleted energy banks. Yet many people have the strange notion that their internal batteries are better recharged by resting. Of course, there are times when the body needs to rest and recuperate, but movement is vital to the recharging process in all of us.

# Exercise 2

## *The Warm-Up*

The Warm-Up is an exercise to raise your core body temperature, activate your circulatory system, and get the blood flowing effectively. Generally, the warm-up is a good practice to do before beginning any other type of physical activity. A proper warm-up will get the blood flowing to the extremities and raise your body temperature by at least one or two degrees. Imagine starting a car on an icy cold day in the middle of winter. You don't immediately put it in gear and start driving. It needs to warm up. The engine oil has not had time to circulate through the engine block. The lack of lubrication puts unnecessary strain on the engine, and there is a good chance you can damage your car. Now, imagine your body as the engine. A proper warm-up provides it with the lubrication needed to prepare it effectively for whatever you plan to do. Of course, it is of great value to focus on deep breathing while doing the warm-up.

The warm-up is practiced from a standing position and consists of five phases: shoulder shrug, shoulder rotation, hip rotation, hip twist, and shaking.

### The Shoulder Shrug

Stand with feet shoulder-width apart. Unlock your knees, gently curl your hips under you, tuck your chin, and straighten your back.

From this relaxed standing position, raise your shoulders up in a simple shrugging motion and then drop them down. Repeat this in a smooth and continuous motion, up and down. Loosen up the muscles of the shoulders. There should be no tension in your arms, and they should wiggle loosely around you as you shrug. Continue for at least ten shrugs. This will help to release the stress and tension that builds up in your shoulders and neck, allowing for better circulation to the brain. Practice this every single day when you wake up.

## Shoulder Rotation

From the same standing position, begin to rotate your shoulders in a gentle circular motion, taking care not to strain yourself. Circle ten times in one direction and then reverse the motion. This type of rotation loosens tension in your joints, enabling the blood to flow smoothly and without obstruction. It lubricates the entire joint with synovial fluid, the body's natural lubricant. Joints often stiffen up because of poor circulation, and this lubrication allows them to function more smoothly and easily. As always, breathing is very important when practicing rotations. Linking the breath to the body movement keeps you aware and present during the exercise. Practice this every single day when you wake up.

## Hip Rotation

Stand with your feet shoulder-width apart and place one hand on each of your hips. Begin to rotate your hips around in a smooth circular motion as if you were using a hula hoop. Move slowly and gently until you become used to the motion. Continue for five or ten rotations and then reverse and rotate in the opposite direction. Continue to go slowly and smoothly as you get the kinks out of your hips. Practice this every single day when you wake up.

## Hip Twist

In contrast to hip rotation this exercise is about moving the hips in a swiveling motion. Stand again with your feet shoulder-width apart, keeping your knees slightly bent. Swivel your hips to one side allowing the arms to follow. Immediately twist the hips back to the other side, letting the arms swing freely. Continue the motion at least ten times. There should be no tension in the arms as they flop around the body. Move smoothly without forcing the movement. Practice this every single day when you wake up.

## Shaking

Stand with your feet shoulder-width apart. Hold your arms in front of you, bent at the elbow and relaxed. Imagine your hands are covered with water and you simply want to shake it off. Begin slowly and then gradually increase speed. Feel as if all the tension in your hands is being shaken off. Be sure to keep them loose and relaxed. Shake for a count of twenty. Stop and let your hands hang down. See if you can notice a tingling in the fingertips. This is the energy moving through your body. Next, shift the weight to one leg and lift the other up and begin shaking it. Shake for a count of ten and then switch to the other side. Stop and try to become aware of the energy moving through your legs. At the risk of sounding repetitive . . . practice this every single day when you wake up.

With a proper warm-up every morning you should start your day feeling awake and invigorated. Your body is now ready to work with you as a partner as you start to delve deeper into reconnecting to the Earth.

# Rebalancing the Mind

With the body as an ally, we can now continue on this life-changing journey. The next aspect of ourselves to work on is our mind. The mind is the element in each of us that enables us to be aware of the world and our experiences. It allows us to think and feel. It is the faculty of consciousness and thought. As we get more in tune with ourselves and the world, we often become aware of the almost incessant internal noise that afflicts all our waking and sometimes our sleeping hours. It is something most people are rarely consciously aware of. This noise is the sound of our own mind as it maintains a never-ending babble during every moment of our daily life.

*"I'm hungry.*

*What's this?*

*Who's that?*

*Oh, my back itches.*

*Where am I going?*

*Is that a potato?*

*Did I leave the light on?*

*How do I look?*

*Ha ha, that's funny.*

*I don't think this is right.*

*Oh, look a bird.*

*Turn left.*

*Wait, what was I thinking about?*

*La dee da."*

This noise is a voice that rattles continuously around in our heads offering us a running commentary on our life and life in general. It tells us what to think. It even tells us what it thinks other people are thinking and what to think about what it thinks other people are thinking! It tells us what we like and don't like. It replays songs, conversations, and thoughts over and over. And worst of all, it reads and repeats every advertisement you see.

This internal noise can be psychologically disruptive because we don't want to imagine that our mind is not under our control. It is often much easier to let our self be drowned out than to try to make sense of our own internal noise. Sadly, the actions we take against it are usually counterproductive. We talk, hoping our spoken words will drown out the inner ones. We put on the TV or listen to music or news to distract us, but this only creates more noise.

# Silence

The first step in the process of rebalancing our mind is learning to be comfortable in silence, or at least to take a break from *external* noise. External noise can fracture our concentration. By quieting our external surroundings we lay the groundwork for perceiving more clearly and coping more effectively with our *internal* noise. External noise is a significant barrier to living life at a slower, more natural pace. In silence, we are able to gather the scattered dimensions of our identity and bring them back to the center of our being. External noise affects us continually. It is made up of all the sounds that we encounter in daily life. It contributes to our internal noise, since every sound we are exposed to is heard by our subconscious and stored in our memory to become a resource for the mind to incorporate into the web it has woven around our spirit. Silencing the external noise and centering our self is the first step and results in a more encompassing state of relaxation.

Sound, of course, is an integral part of life, but it can also be a hindrance to exploring our deeper being. Concentration is difficult when we are being bombarded with noise that tends to divert our attention and distract us from the more important things in life. And there is plenty of unnecessary noise in the world today. Only by learning ways to manage the external noise around us can we begin to feel a sense of peacefulness and serenity that prepares us to deal with the inner noise.

Some people are significantly bothered by silence, needing, for example, to have the television on continuously when they are alone in order to feel comfortable. Or when they are with other people they often talk just to fill a silence that makes them feel anxious. Why is silence uncomfortable? It shouldn't be, given that it offers a rich opportunity to examine the inner self. But that may be the very reason for feeling anxious. Exploring the deeper self, or at least being suddenly highly conscious of it, can be frightening if you are uncertain of who you really are and what you are doing here. This fear can become very powerful as you plumb the deeper reaches of your being, but what the fear is actually doing is opening a path to self-discovery. It is opening you to truths about yourself that have been obscured by all the external noise. The fact that you are beginning to look inside yourself is part of the definition of who you are. The more you explore, the more you begin to discover and identify your deeper self.

Try it.

# Exercise 3

## *External Silence*

This is an exercise to bring a little more silence into your life. Whenever it is most convenient for you, in the morning, afternoon, or evening, allow yourself ten minutes to be totally silent. Find a secluded space somewhere you will not be disturbed by the phone or the children or whatever it is that distracts you. Try to schedule it at the same time each day. During this silent time there should be no sounds—no television, no talking, no phone—just complete silence. See if you can find one moment where there is absolutely no sound at all. I realize that in today's bustling world this is often difficult if not impossible, but you at least have to give it a try. Honestly, if you cannot find ten minutes of quiet time for yourself, it's probably too late. However, once you have practiced finding ten minutes a day for a week or so, you will begin to notice the feelings that emerge during your silent time. At first I'm sure you will be distracted by the multitude of thoughts that seem to appear in your mind uninvited. Do you tell yourself that sitting here is stupid and you should go do something? Who is telling you that it is stupid? Is it possible that part of your mind does not want you to discover what can be heard in silence?

As you progress, see if you can make silent time a regular routine. Adapt as you need to. If the morning is too busy or noisy, try it in the evening. If you drive in your car with the radio or music on all the time, try driving in silence. Do whatever you need to do in order to make it a comfortable and enjoyable experience. Plug your ears if necessary. Get used to silence. For many people, programming a period of silence may seem silly. For others, the silence can be a little daunting. But don't allow yourself to be sidetracked. Almost anyone can benefit by bringing more silence into their daily life.

As we will discover in the next section, silence can be used as a tool to help us explore our deeper self and our connection to the Earth. Silence is the place to start to experience more fully who we are and how we fit into the larger scheme of things. Sitting like this in silence is a form of meditation. It is a contemplation of your self and your place in the universe.

For people who have had no experience with meditation, the word can have negative religious connotations. However, one does not have to be religious or even interested in religion to find value in this simple, profound practice. Meditation is simply the most effective technique for calming the internal noise of the mind. It is a method for developing concentration, enhancing self-understanding, and calming the mind's unbidden thoughts. Becoming more aware of your self and realizing your spiritual nature is something that transcends religion. Anyone who has explored meditation even a little realizes that it is merely a path that leads to a new, more expansive way of seeing the world around us.

*When the mind wanders, accept it. Then bring it home.*
*When the mind chatters, accept it. Then quieten it.*
*When the mind is unconscious, accept it. Then awaken it.*
*Your mind may not believe everything you tell it,*
*but it thrives and survives on what you feed it.*
*What are you feeding your mind?*
—*Shanti Gowans*

Used with permission, © Shanti Gowans

Of course, meditation can be a challenge. If we imagine our mind as a hyperactive monkey that is continuously chattering but saying very little of any value, we can begin to understand the problem. Without an effective way to quiet the mind's yammering it is very difficult to move onto what our spirit is trying to tell us. It gets drowned out. Many of today's problems such as stress, depression, obsession, anxiety, and, yes, addiction are all created from thoughts that have taken control of the mind. Even though we may know these thoughts are detrimental, we believe there is nothing we can do to counter them. But that is not true. We simply need an effective method of concentrating and training the mind to be an ally instead of an enemy.

## Exercise 4

### *Cultivating Quietism*

Finding or creating internal silence can be challenging. The mind is simply not used to being peaceful. When things do calm down, we often look immediately for some new distraction. Cultivating quietism is a method for occupying the mind while, at the same time, allowing it to settle down of its own accord.

Like a glass of muddy water that has been shaken up and then set aside, quietism is a state of mind that results from letting the brain's detritus sink to the bottom, leaving the mind clear and pure. Quietism is a state of calmness unfazed by the rapid pace of the world around you and the myriad of unbidden thoughts that vie for attention. It is a state of peace and tranquility that enables you to relax and enjoy the sense of your inner and outer selves being in tune with each other.

We all understand that an integral relationship with nature is a fundamental dimension of human existence. Without it, we lose a sense of the interconnectedness of all living things and the physical and mental sustenance they provide. The trees, grass, mountains, oceans, and animals of the world contain the essence of life, and to deny ourselves exposure to them is to deprive our being of what it needs to be an inherent part of the natural world, to be a part of the Earth.

Quietism is an important step in the nature-based training of healing our relationship with nature. The intent of quietism is not to clear thoughts entirely from the mind. Instead, it is to focus your thoughts and attention on a natural scene or setting so intensely that your usual patterns of thinking are interrupted or temporarily redirected. You are not attempting to stifle the inner voice, but simply to cultivate a state of such total concentration that the unwanted thoughts cannot successfully intrude or take control of the quiet domain you are creating. This is done by concentrating your thoughts and focusing your senses on a natural setting and then directing all your attention to it.

See if you can find one of the environments of quietism described below. Seat yourself comfortably and begin your observation. Observe the setting as a whole as well as running your eyes over each part of it. Listen to it as well—and smell it, touch it, and taste it if you can.

Once you have immersed yourself in the environment, go to your breathing.

Don't forget: breathing is fundamental. Use the breath to connect with the environment. Use the breath to connect you with your self.

Try to identify the essence or essential nature of the environment *and absorb it into your own sense of being.* Experience the feeling of peaceful relaxation you are cultivating as you expand yourself.

Just relax . . . and breathe.

## ENVIRONMENTS FOR OBSERVATION

# Day Sky

The day sky is deep and clear. The clouds bring movement and change. Time slows down as the clouds drift slowly by. Become aware of their subtle movement and change in form as they drift above you. If you imagine each cloud as an occasional intruding thought, let it pass by and move on. Release the mind and let it be free within the vast confines of the sky and all that is there.

# Night Sky

The night sky presents the quality of silent eternity. The stars and constellations hint at the vastness of the cosmos. Different stars and constellations appear with the changing seasons. Calmly observe the stars and the moon as they wander across the night sky. The moon embodies a magical strength and mystery. Let the mind expand to fill the heavens, and all other thoughts are quickly and easily let go.

# Ocean

The ocean is immense and ever changing. It is continuously moving, yet from a distance appears still. The ocean reflects the mind. It is deep and mysterious. Let the waves match your breath as they wash onto the shore in a continuous, never-ending motion. Listen to the sound of the waves. Let the sound wash over you. Exist within that moment.

# Running Water

The continuous movement of running water reflects the mind. Stopping the flow of water is like trying to stop the thoughts of the mind. It is better to redirect the thoughts to places where we want them to go than to fight against the relentless flow. Allow the mind to *become* water. Let it flow through your being.

# Mountains

Mountains contain the essence of the Earth's strength. Feel the massive solidity of the mountain. It cannot be moved. Strength and solidity are deeply embedded in the Earth. Feel the mountain within you and allow the mind to be solid as the mountain, unfazed by petty thoughts and emotions. Feel yourself grounded and connected to the Earth, solid and stable.

# Trees

The life cycle of a tree reflects the cycle of all life. From seed to sapling to mature tree to dead wood, the tree passes through the cycle as we all do. Each tree is unique and embodies the essence of life. Roots sink deep into the Earth. Imagine the wind as a wave of discursive thought. The tree does not fight against the wind, instead it moves with the wind, swaying back and forth allowing the wind to pass through. Bring that feeling within yourself.

# Fire

Fire contains warmth and vitality. Yet its erratic and wild movement reflects the mind's penchant for flitting from one thought to another in rapid succession. It is difficult to focus on a single point of flame. Don't focus the eyes; instead, simply let them relax and follow the movement of the flame. Let the mind flow with the dance of the fire. Feel the glow of the fire within you.

# Anywhere and Everywhere

People who live in big cities may often feel that access to natural settings is rare or spoiled. But quietism settings can be found anywhere. Parks, gardens, and rooftops all offer opportunities to cultivate peace within.

Take the time to breathe and relax whenever possible. Nature exists all around us; we just rarely take the time to experience it. Stop. Breathe. Relax and enjoy it. This practice allows your mind to free itself of its habitual thought patterns and opens up infinite possibilities.

At its core, all meditation practice is about touching the spiritual essence that exists within us all. The spiritual essence is not something that we create through meditation. It is already there, deep within, behind all the barriers, patiently waiting for us to recognize it. Our spirit is held captive by our mind. It is waiting to be liberated and given a chance to help us discover our true self and connect to all things.

# Reconnecting Practice

## Advice from a Tree®

*Dear Friend,*
*Stand Tall and Proud*
*Sink your roots deeply into the Earth*
*Reflect the light of a greater source*
*Think long term*
*Go out on a limb*
*Remember your place among all living beings*
*Embrace with joy the changing seasons*
*For each yields its own abundance*
*The Energy and Birth of Spring*
*The Growth and Contentment of Summer*
*The Wisdom to let go of leaves in the Fall*
*The Rest and Quiet Renewal of Winter*
*Feel the wind and the sun*
*And delight in their presence*
*Look up at the moon that shines down upon you*
*And the mystery of the stars at night*
*Seek nourishment from the good things in life*
*Simple pleasures: Earth, fresh air, light*
*Be content with your natural beauty*
*Drink plenty of water*
*Let your limbs sway and dance in the breezes*
*Be flexible*
*Remember your roots*

*Enjoy the view!*

*—Ilan Shamir*

Used with permission © Ilan Shamir
2018 yourtruenature.com

# Reconnecting to Spirit

It would probably be more accurate to call this process "Remembering our Connection to Spirit." As I said earlier, we are all connected within the intricate web of existence. Even if we are not aware of the connection, we are still connected. Each of us is affected by the actions of others. Everything is interrelated; nothing exists in isolation. The idea of an intricate web-like structure connecting all things is not new. The concept of a web that connects all life has been used by philosophers, poets, and mystics throughout the millennia to describe that interconnectedness. Similar concepts are found in diverse traditions, both ancient and modern, throughout the world. It makes no difference from what angle it is viewed, ancient or modern, spiritual, religious, philosophical, or even scientific, the idea remains fundamentally the same: there is something that connects us with everything else in existence. While each of the various different views may define or describe this whole in differing terms, it always ends up resembling a network of interwoven strands creating a universal interdependence among all things.

All living things are connected by the life force that flows through them. If you can imagine this connection as billions and billions of tiny web-like fibers linking all things in creation, you can begin to visualize how we are intertwined. We are made up of the life-force energy that is part of everything. And every living thing is part of the whole. The plants and animals of the world including humans all have a relationship to one another. At the most basic level this is obvious. It is no accident that the oxygen we breathe is a byproduct of the plants as they go through the life process of photosynthesis, just as the carbon dioxide we exhale is exactly what plants require to live.

# Connection

Your Spirit is your connection to the whole. It is the part of you that is linked to all other life on the planet. It is an interactive connection on a profound level. When you become aware of it, and begin to explore your connection to the life force of the other beings on the planet, you begin to feel your life filling with deeper meaning. It is like passing through a door that leads to a whole other world and way of living. By immersing yourself into the connection you can begin to cultivate a relationship with everything. Your Spirit wants that connection. It thrives on the mutual exchange of energy the Earth provides. All you have to do is consciously realize your connection to it.

# Exercise 5

## *Go Outside*

Really.

I mean it.

Go outside and stay there for a while.

There is absolutely no possible way you can connect yourself to the Spirit within you if you are not in touch with the natural world around you. The other beings of this planet make your Spirit whole. Beginning to cultivate a relationship with the various plants, animals, birds, and insects allows you access to that part of you that is connected to the whole. In order to realize your connection to it, you need make yourself available for it to connect with you. The only way to do this is to actually go out in nature and interact with it. Go outside and take some time to observe the dance of life around you. Open yourself to the possibility that everything around you is flowing to the rhythm of life. Let the wind blow through your hair. Take off your shoes and walk barefoot in the grass. Climb a tree. Ask yourself if there could be more to the world than the confines of your own personal thoughts and experiences.

Do this practice on a daily basis. Our connection to the Earth is reinforced through repetitive contact with the natural world. Open yourself to the potential. The Earth wants you to remember. All that is stopping you is you.

# Immersion

Perhaps you already have a committed breathing and movement practice like yoga or tai chi. Perhaps you avidly pursue outdoor activities. Perhaps you are a teacher of the mental or physical arts. That is absolutely wonderful. Now, it is simply time to take it further. Wherever you are on your journey, it is now time to move deeper. It is time to strengthen your connection to the Earth and build on what you have already accomplished. Our connection grows stronger and stronger the more we practice and reinforce it. Spending time outside, breathing, and getting to truly know the energies of the plants and animals of the world enhances the connection. It is the same principle as with practicing anything. The more you do something, the better you get at it. Start to make personal relationships with individual beings. Get to know a specific tree. Sit with your back resting against it and have a conversation with it. Trees don't often respond, except with the occasional creak or a rustling of leaves in the wind, but they are really good listeners.

## Exercise 6

### *Nodding to Everything*

Nodding to everything is a process of acknowledgment. It is a way to help cultivate a relationship with the nonhuman beings of the planet. As you become mindful of your place in the world, nodding to everything becomes a very special practice to begin to recognize the Spirit within you as well as in all the other things around you. A nod of the head toward something can be thought of as a sign of respect as you are consciously acknowledging the inherent life force within all things. It is a way to express gratitude for the energy everything contributes to the world. At the same time, nodding to everything allows you to soften and gives you a chance to discover the beauty and goodness in all things.

As you spend more time outside, begin to notice individual beings. They can be trees, bushes, rocks, bugs, birds, or any part of the natural world. Observe them and give a nod of acknowledgment. You can even say "hi" if you are so inclined. The purpose of this exercise is to get more comfortable interacting with the nonhuman beings of the planet.

# Reconnecting to the Soul

*Get out of your head and get into your heart. Think less, feel more.*

*—Osho*

Your soul is that deep inner core of your being that sets you apart from everyone and everything else. To recover your soul is to find your true self. The soul holds your individuality together and creates your identity. It is that part of you that is completely unique from every other being on the planet. Because each individual's soul is like no other, the path to a realization of the soul is an intensely personal experience. Reconnecting to the soul is certainly a profound experience, but it can also be both lonely and frightening. It is easy to be overwhelmed by the emotional aspect of truly looking at yourself. Many people have deep wounds from traumatic experiences they have gone through. Reconnecting to the soul can bring up childhood traumas that have not been resolved. Even people who think themselves relatively stable may uncover things they may not even have realized they were carrying with them.

The only way forward is to go through the process. If you are truly looking for meaning in your life, this is a journey you must embark on. Go slow and take your time. This is your life's work.

# Exercise 7

## *Finding Your Purpose*

Finding your purpose is done through introspection. Introspection is the examination of one's own conscious thoughts and feelings. It is a method of self-reflection to determine one's emotional, sensory, and cognitive mental states. Uncovering your life's purpose through introspection is like gathering the various pieces of yourself together, so you can then assemble the puzzle of who you truly are. Your purpose will eventually become the driving force of your life. Your purpose is your connection to something larger, something that will allow you to truly make a difference in the world.

For this exercise you will need a notebook or journal. Writing in a journal is a useful tool for making any changes to your life or your perspective since you are able to track your changes as you progress. Creating a dedicated journal for this exercise will help you understand and explore your thoughts about your life's purpose, your passions, and your joys.

Try to answer each question as fully and in-depth as possible. Be as honest as you can be with yourself. There are no right or wrong answers to these questions. No one else ever needs to look at your answers.

Step 1.
Answer the following questions in as much detail as possible. Turn off your self-judgment and write whatever comes to mind.

If you had unlimited money, how would you spend your day?
How would you describe your perfect day?
What activities touch your soul?
What do you truly love to do?

Step 2.
Answer the following questions as you think back to your childhood, when your life was freer, more playful, and more alive.

What brought you joy as a child?
What were you doing when you lost track of time?
What activities did your parents have to drag you away from?
What did you truly love?

Step 3.
Expand your reflections by answering the following questions.

When have you been happiest in your life?
What has made you truly proud of yourself?
What qualities do you most admire in other people?
What makes you feel really alive and energized?
How happy are you on a daily basis?
If you had one week to live, how would you spend that week?
If you could change one thing about the world, what would it be?
What one change could make your life happier?

Step 4.
The answers to all of the questions above should give you a clearer idea as to what your purpose in life might be. Do you see a pattern within your answers? Is there something that stands out?

Next, write your personal mission statement. Try to frame it in a format that gives you focus and direction in order for you to move forward. An active, actionable personal mission statement allows you to set a goal and gives you the means for heading in that direction. Once you have your statement, begin to set your intentions. Focus on the goal and see it coming to fruition. Clear your mind and picture your life the way you'd like for it to be.

Step 5.
Finally, make a list of positive actions that will lead you toward your purpose. This can be a list of direct actions that you can take or it might be short-term actions that are steps on the path you need to take to eventually reach your purpose. Become aware of behaviors or actions that no longer help you move in that direction. You probably no longer need them. Let go of the things that are of no use. Then

follow your path.

# Delving Deeper

Let me be perfectly clear. Once you have started on this path, it is difficult to go back to the world of ignorance. You start to vibrate on a different level. The old world will start to feel more and more alien and uncomfortable. You may not relate to certain people who are still caught up in distraction. Activities that you used to enjoy may lose their appeal as you find they don't really bring any satisfaction. You might suddenly find daily life is too loud and disruptive. It can make you feel disoriented and overwhelmed by the assault on your senses. This is a difficult part of the process, but there is no going back. The only way to go is forward, and forward means going deeper within yourself.

## Exercise 8

### *Seclusion*

It is now time to take things to a deeper level. In order to do this exercise, you will need to set aside a twenty-four-hour time period when you have no distractions, no commitments, and no obligations. I realize that this can be a challenge in today's busy world, but sometimes you need to make time for things that are simply too important. Make the time for this; you will be grateful to yourself.

Once you have your block of time set aside you will need to find a sacred space. The basic idea of this exercise is for you to spend the whole twenty-four hours outside in quiet solitude. The Japanese call this practice *shinrin-yoku*, which literally translates to "taking in the forest atmosphere" or "forest bathing" and refers to the process of soaking up the sights, smells, and sounds of a natural setting to promote physiological and psychological health. During this time, you will be totally immersed in the natural world. This means no interaction or contact with any other human being. This exercise often works best if you set up your sacred space in advance. Mark out an area that feels comfortable to you. It can be as large or small as necessary, but most likely it should be no bigger than 10 feet x 10 feet. Set up a tent, hammock, or whatever you feel is necessary for protection from the elements. It is important to stay safe and relatively comfortable, but you really will need to commit to the full time secluded in nature. Bring some food and water, but only enough to sustain yourself. This is not a time of indulgence.

Once you are immersed and secluded, start to take notice of the world around you. Twenty-four hours is a long time for many people when there is no one else around and especially without technological stimulation. Instead, you will have to use your hands and feet to make contact with the Earth. You will need to talk to the plants and animals you encounter as you become an integral part of the natural world you are immersed in. You are now cultivating your connection to the Earth.

This is your time.

Embrace it.

# Chapter 4
## The Sevens:
## Creating a Sustainable Practice

### Mistwalkers

*There are those who spend their day*

*Living in a different way*

*Apart from all the hectic noise*

*Away from shows and ads and toys*

*Away from stores and shops and such*

*They have enough, they don't need much*

*They touch the soul of Mother Earth*

*They live in peace and joy and mirth*

*In their hearts, no room for fear*

*Their eyes are bright, their thoughts are clear*

*Each step they take the ground is kissed*

*These walkers in the sacred mist*

*—Aaron Hoopes*

Reconnecting to the Earth is not something that you do once and then forget about. Nor is it something you do at a specific time each day or week. Developing a sustainable practice is a continuing process of personal growth and development throughout your whole life. It is something that grows and evolves continuously all the time no matter what else you are doing. This is truly a journey both inward as well as outward. It is a chance for discovering the true perfection that resides within you and in the world around you. Merging the inner and outer worlds completes your being. It gives you a sense of wholeness. When you focus on these practices, you lay the fertile ground for a profound transformation to take place. As your practice is integrated into your daily life, it becomes a part of you. As you progress, you will begin to realize that reconnecting to the Earth is not something you learn, but something you become. It is the remembering of who you truly are.

The Sevens are seven sets of seven fundamental principles and guidelines for realizing this transformation. They are designed to assist you in creating a committed personal practice that will deepen your connection to both nature and yourself. Use them to assist you on your journey.

# The Seven Stages

The first of the Sevens are related to our growing awareness of the state of the planet. There really cannot be any doubt that humans have done significant damage to the planet. Resources are rapidly becoming scarce as we consume more and more. Large areas of the Earth are now contaminated and virtually uninhabitable. The oceans have been our dumping grounds for way too long. The repercussions from the disasters like the Fukushima meltdown will be with us longer than we can imagine. Coming to terms with this destruction is vital if we are going to move forward.

The seven stages are similar to the stages that anyone goes through when dealing with a traumatic situation. In starting the process of reconnecting with the Earth, we must go through these stages to enable us to awaken to the state of the world. Those of us already doing the work on ourselves need to be aware of the stages so that we can assist others as they navigate them.

# 1. Oblivion

If you are reading these words, I think it would be safe to say that you have successfully moved beyond stage one, and in fact, you may already be deep into stage seven. Nevertheless, stage one is oblivion, a state of unconscious ignorance.

Oblivion is the stage of being so plugged into the mainstream consumer society that you are completely unable or unwilling to even look at the possibility that the human race is causing irrevocable damage to the planet. People in this stage go about their business never really even considering the ramifications of their behavior.

# 2. Shock and Denial

When you are finally first exposed to the state of the planet, be it from an oil spill, a forest clear cut, water contamination, radioactive fallout, a fish/bird dieoff, or any of the hundreds of other horrendous events, the reaction is often one of numbed disbelief. Quite often, the first thing people do when finally breaking out of the oblivion stage is to go into shock and deny the reality of the situation. This is a normal reaction to a horror that reaches deep into the soul. The shock provides emotional protection from being overwhelmed all at once. Then comes a strong desire to rationalize the overwhelming emotions that come from being confronted with that which we don't want to believe. People will go to great lengths to block out truth. It is a defense mechanism that buffers the immediate shock.

People in this stage need to be treated with compassion as this is a temporary response that will carry them through the first waves of pain.

## 3. Pain and Guilt

The truth is that coming to full realization of the extent to which we have devastated the Earth can be a deeply traumatic experience. Pain and guilt usually begin when the numbness of shock and denial wears off and is replaced with real heartfelt suffering. Sometimes this feeling is described as feeling as if you have a hole in your being. At this stage it is important to experience the pain fully, and not hide it, avoid it, or escape from it with drugs, alcohol, or any other addiction. Most likely, at this stage, life begins to feel more chaotic and scarier as emotional pain begins to become overwhelming.

People in this stage can be very emotional and need caring and love.

## 4. Depression

Eventually the pain and guilt lead to a helpless feeling that can turn into depression. Depression is a catch-all phrase that describes a number of mental states. In this case, overwhelming sadness is usually the main experience. During this time, a full realization of the true magnitude of the destruction to the planet becomes apparent. It is naturally depressing. There is a tendency toward isolation at this stage as time is spent reflecting on how things got to this state.

People in this stage experience feelings of emptiness or despair with no hope of relief.

## 5. Anger and Frustration

If one is able to shake off the heavy cloak of depression, reality and its pain reemerge. And, ready or not, that pain can hit like a freight train. In reaction, the intense emotional energy that is generated is deflected from the vulnerable core of the being and redirected outward. This energy is often expressed as anger and frustration. The anger can be aimed at inanimate objects, complete strangers, friends, or family.

People in this stage often lash out with words or actions that can be dangerous. They may not have the ability to temper their emotions and care must be taken to calm them down.

## 6. Acceptance

Eventually the anger and frustration begin to change into something else. Acceptance is the stage when one finally reaches a point where they are ready to accept and deal with the reality of the situation. Acceptance does not necessarily mean a return to happiness. Given the truth of the situation, one can never really return to the carefree, untroubled world that existed before this tragedy was exposed.

People in this stage are ready to begin to try and find a way forward.

## 7. Action

Eventually, a point is reached where critical thinking returns. The harsh pain and sadness are no longer dominating the emotions. Of course, the pain and sadness never really go away, but now there should be the feeling of an energy rising within that is spurring action to do something about the situation. Now is the time to start looking forward and becoming proactive. The only way to deal with the challenges ahead are with a positive outlook and determination to make things different.

People at this stage are ready to make effective changes in their behavior and lifestyles that can make a difference.

Let's begin.

# The Seven Precepts

The process of reconnecting with the Earth can take a lifetime, especially if we are caught up in the mainstream life of this world. The seven precepts represent the fundamental actions we can begin to take to navigate this journey. These seven simple precepts are basic tenants that should be applied to every aspect of your life in order to make it more peaceful and enjoyable regardless of what else you do.

## 1. Slow Down

What's your hurry? Life can run at any pace. It is within you to decide how fast to live your life. Rushing through it only gets you to the end quicker. And there are so many wonderful things that you will miss along the way. "Take your time to stop and smell the roses," as the old saying goes.

In the mainstream world, time is measured by hours, minutes, and seconds. When you are outside in nature these constructs melt away. Clocks have taught you to abandon the natural rhythms of the Earth and your own body. Slowing down is about becoming more present in the moment. The practice of becoming more aware of the present moment is studied by many different disciplines, but the outcome is the same, an intimate connection with all that is happening around you. Outside in nature everything moves at a natural pace according to its own natural rhythm. The sun rises and sets. Trees grow slowly. The seasons change. Your challenge is to stay in the present moment and be aware of the pace of time when you are in nature. There is no hurry.

## 2. Expand Your Heart

We are all on our own journey, and for many it is a difficult and challenging struggle. Learn to be forgiving and accepting of others. They are simply trying to find their own way in this crazy world. Many people are lost and have great difficulty finding the answers to the problems in their lives. Don't make arbitrary judgments about them. Your practice should be learning to accept them as they are—good, bad, or neutral. Offer what you are able to give without compromising your own heart. By giving of your time and energy, you create an inexhaustible source of positive energy that can be passed on and on.

Above all, allow yourself to enjoy life without exception. Smile, laugh, dance, skip, and giggle.

## 3. Nourish Your Body

Your body is your physical presence in this world. Under the most ideal circumstances it might live for a hundred years or so. Unfortunately, with all of the toxins, poisons, and chemicals in the air, food, and water we consume, "ideal circumstances" are not usually an option. By becoming proactive and taking conscious steps to care for your body, you are giving it the best opportunity to thrive in less-than-optimal conditions.

Eating healthy food is a major part of body nourishment and would take another whole book to address; however, locally grown, organic food should be a major portion of anyone's diet if they want to stay healthy. Clean, fresh water is also of vital importance.

Another method for nourishing the body is, of course, conscious, mindful deep breathing. This is the simplest, yet most beneficial thing you can do for yourself. Bringing fresh oxygen and energy into your body fills it with the elixir it needs to flourish. It takes very little effort, simply a desire to change your routine and a conscious effort to remember to breathe. Practice this every day. Give your body what it needs.

## 4. Calm Your Mind

Relaxation is more than physical. It is about stilling the torrent of thoughts that run rampant in your head. Remember the handful of dirt thrown into a glass of water and shaken up? The result is a glass of swirling muddy water. If you set that glass aside, the dirt will slowly settle to the bottom and the water will become clear again. Imagine your mind is the glass of water and the dirt represents the myriad of thoughts that are vying for attention. You can deal with it in the same manner. Sitting quietly and allowing your thoughts to settle will result in clarity.

Your mind can be a powerful tool for positive change in this world. When you teach it to follow you, as opposed to you following it, you create an energy field of intention. Of course, this takes a lot of practice since your mind has had your whole life up until now to run free. If you spend the time and effort to reign it in, you will be rewarded with the ability to think clearly and make the right decisions. Be patient and determined and you will find your way.

## 5. Cultivate Your Spirit

Begin to build your relationship with all of the other beings on the planet. Spend time outside interacting with the plants and animals. Work to fully understand that humans are simply one of the many different species that share this beautiful planet. By creating a relationship with the other beings of the planet, you expand your circle and open yourself up to an endless vista of possibilities. Your spirit thrives on the connection to the Earth. Allow it to be immersed. You are not alone . . . give yourself permission to become part of the whole and for the whole to become part of you.

## 6. Honor Your Soul

Your soul is unique among all things in this universe. Recognize and accept that you are special. Your realization of your own soul opens up a whole new dimension of your self. Imagine your soul as a tiny caterpillar deep within you. These types of practices that help you connect with yourself, such as conscious breathing and mindful awareness of the present moment, are the chrysalis your soul needs to develop. Care for and nurture your soul and eventually that tiny caterpillar will transform into a beautiful butterfly with a magnificent set of wings to carry you wherever you need to go. Do not be afraid of finding your true self. Allow yourself to shine like a star in the heavens.

## 7. Love Yourself and the Earth

You are the only one who is with you from the moment you are born to the day you die. To go through life not loving yourself is total foolishness. You are the only one who can give that love to yourself. Realize your perfection and accept the love.

At the same time, it is vital to realize that the Earth gives us everything we need for life. We cannot treat is as a garbage dump. We must cherish it as sacred. As you move toward an understanding of your place on the Earth, you will learn to love it as deeply as you are able. Don't just grasp this idea with your intellect; realize it within your body, mind, spirit, and soul.

# The Seven Qualities

The seven qualities are attitudes we need to embody as we make our way through the challenges and experiences of this life. We all need some guiding principles to live by. The seven qualities reflect us at our best. We may not always be perfect but keeping them in our thoughts gives us something to aspire toward.

## 1. Gentle Kindness

This is self-explanatory. Being gentle and kind is not a hard concept to understand. Gentle kindness is a way of being. It is a state of mind in which you greet everyone and everything you meet with a smile and a gentle touch. Gentle kindness is being nice. It's really that simple. Cultivate a willingness to offer your help to others in need. By being sincere in your heart and open to giving of your time and energy, you create a two-way dialogue with the universe that brings that energy back to you.

## 2. Respect

Respect is a feeling or understanding that someone or something is important or serious and should be treated in an appropriate manner. On a practical level, respect includes taking someone's feelings, needs, thoughts, ideas, wishes, and preferences into consideration. It means taking all of these seriously and giving them worth and value. In fact, giving someone respect seems similar to valuing them and their thoughts, feelings, etc. It also includes acknowledging them, listening to them, being truthful with them, and accepting their individuality and idiosyncrasies. Respect can be shown through behavior and it can also be felt. We can act in ways that are considered respectful, yet we can also feel respect for someone and feel respected by someone. In nature, respect is the process of honoring everything's right to exist. At the very least it is a way of acknowledging the understanding that all things are connected. Truly valuing things enriches all life.

## 3. Generosity

Generosity is the virtue of giving good things to others freely and abundantly without expecting anything in return. Generosity always intends to enhance the true well-being of those to whom it is given. It can involve offering time, assets, or talents to aid someone in need. Generosity is based on pure intentions of looking out for the common good and giving from the heart. In nature, generosity is about giving back our energy to the world.

## 4. Honesty

Honesty is a facet of moral character and connotes positive and virtuous attributes such as truthfulness and straightforwardness. It implies the absence of lying, cheating, and theft. Furthermore, honesty means being trustworthy, loyal, fair, and sincere. When we are honest in every way, we are able to enjoy peace of mind and maintain self-respect. We build strength of character that allows us to grow stronger.

## 5. *Integrity*

Integrity is the quality of having strong moral principles. It is a state of moral uprightness that is a personal choice to hold oneself to consistently moral and ethical standards. Integrity means being honest and keeping your word. It means doing the right things at all times in all circumstances, whether or not anyone is watching. It takes courage to do the right thing, no matter the consequences. A person with integrity draws others to them because they are trustworthy and dependable.

## 6. *Adaptability*

Adaptability is the ability to change or be changed to fit changed circumstances. It is the ability to alter oneself to fit to new circumstances. It can also be seen as the ability to cope with unexpected disturbances in one's environment. Adaptability is predominantly about flexibility in fluid situations. In times of change, it is important to be flexible and open to new ideas. As we get more in tune with the Earth, change is going to be a constant companion. It is vital to be able to go with the flow of events. That way you can adjust yourself as necessary in order to thrive.

## 7. *Equanimity*

Equanimity is the capacity to maintain a state of internal calmness at all times regardless of the circumstances. It is the practice of keeping your composure in good times and bad. Equanimity is a state of mental stability and composure that is undisturbed by experiences that may be painful or difficult. In stressful situations when anxiety is high, equanimity provides clarity and strength to deal with the challenges you face. It is a virtue that prevents self-destruction when blamed, but also avoids false pride when praised. Equanimity guides us to be present in the moment and not be overcome by passions, desires, or emotions.

# The Seven Experiences

The Seven Experiences are what this process of reconnecting to the Earth provides us on a deep, fundamental level. When we are in tune with the vibrations of the whole and connected to all the beings on the planet we are able to experience a life full of meaning and joy. Each of us will go through the seven experiences in one form or another. The more open and willing we are as we undergo this process, the more profound each experience will be.

## 1. Life

Life is something we share with each and every being on the planet. Becoming aware of the grand mystery of life is a significant step in each person's evolution. As we connect to the Earth, it becomes even more intense. In nature, we can see the ebb and flow of life as the grass grows and the buds on the trees expand into leaves. If you watch a caterpillar build a chrysalis and transform into a butterfly, you cannot help but feel a magical connection to the process of life. Life is an experience we must fully embrace. We have been blessed with this opportunity to experience it. We need to step into life and live it fully.

## 2. Death

Death is part of the natural process of life. It may be an uncomfortable subject to those who are not fully living their lives, but the truth is that everyone needs to accept and become comfortable with the concept of death. We are all going to die. There is no way to avoid it. Everyone around you is going to die as well. What is important is what you make of the time you have here, alive on this planet. In reality, death is merely a transformation. It is part of a grand cycle. Nature provides you with examples of this all the time. It is in the cycle of the seasons as winter comes and the leaves fall from the trees. By observing the experience of death in the natural world, you come face to face with the natural cycle of life and death. Then you will begin to value your own life more. As you become more in tune to the Earth and exist more in the present moment, you will begin to experience the true joy of being alive, while understanding death is a natural part of the process.

## 3. Love

Love is usually thought of as a variety of attitudes and feelings related to attraction and affection. However, love can also be a virtue representing a kind and compassionate attitude toward other beings on the planet. As part of the Earth, we are accepted just as we are. We are integrated into the whole. Spending time in nature expands our feelings of love. Nature has no opinions about your behavior. It makes no judgments about how you look or the way you act. Nature gives you the opportunity to truly learn to love unconditionally. It provides the inspiration that allows your heart to soar and joy to radiate from your being. Nature is the true embodiment of love.

## 4. Enough

Sadly, our culture teaches us that we never have enough. We strive to make more money, buy more things, eat more food, watch more shows, and fill up every corner of ourselves with more and more and more and more and more. Even when we have plenty, the urge for more is hard to resist. We have been conditioned from childhood to want more. It is a difficult habit to break. But enough is enough. It is time to do something different. The more in tune with the natural world we become, the easier it is to decide when we've had enough. The natural world provides many examples with its ecosystems that embody harmony and balance. Trees grow to a height that reflects the nutrients and water available in their immediate space. Squirrels store the right amount of food to get them through the winter. It is time for us to learn to recognize when we have had enough of something. In this manner we may finally be fulfilled.

## 5. *Beauty*

Beauty is a characteristic of someone or something that provides a perceptual experience of pleasure for the observer. Beauty often involves an interpretation of something being in balance and harmony with nature. The stunning majesty of a mountain rising up out of the Earth, the miracle of a flower infused with sunlight, being visited by a bee on its journey to gather sustenance, the power of a tree rooted in the Earth and stretching to the sky all convey a sense of beauty. The natural world allows you to feel the beauty and awe of the world. Nature provides a deep sense of joy in the experience of beauty in all its incarnations.

## 6. *The Self*

The self is made up of a number of areas in our lives. Our abilities, affiliations, relationships, family, and occupation all give us a sense of self. A strong sense of self can overcome nearly any obstacle. Our beliefs about ourselves have a tremendous amount to do with what ends up happening to us, what we accomplish, and the quality of our life. Inside each and every one of us there needs to be an understanding of who we are. Our sense of self underlies our internal strength as human beings, and it enables us to accomplish what we desire. Having a powerful sense of self can make all the difference in life. Nature gives us the opportunity to truly experience the self. When immersed in the natural world, we feel our connection to the Earth. We become a part of the community of nature. In nature, everything is made of the same energy and has a place. Nature allows us to get comfortable in our own skin as we experience the truth of our own being.

## 7. The Divine

The divine is considered to be of transcendental origin. It is sometimes considered to be a supernatural power or deity. But it is important to clarify that the divine resides within us all. It is the source of light and life within. It is sacred, holy, and eternal. As you open up to the divine, you enable the manifestation of your highest truth. The divine brings guidance, peace, and harmony. Whether you call the divine Creator, Allah, God, Buddha, Jesus, Earth Mother, Tao, Great Spirit, or any other name makes no difference for they are the same thing. The divine is the essence of the universe. As we reconnect to nature, we entrain with this powerful, loving presence that supports and nourishes us. The true experience is a communion with something greater than our individual self.

# The Seven Directions

In the Native American tradition, the four cardinal directions are usually called either Guardians or Spirit Keepers and are seen as divine beings that work with each direction. These four directions along with the other three directions make up the seven directions. The directions enable you to make the world your sacred place. Take your time and attune to the spirit and power of each direction. Look at the gifts each direction gives you. Learn and appreciate the symbols for each direction. Deepen your relationship with the seven directions and with the whole of life they form together. When you get in touch with these sacred directions with honor, respect, and gratitude, you are given the opportunity to open yourself up to the universal energy.

## 1. East

East is where the sun rises. It symbolizes the dawning of a new day. The eastern spirit of sun or fire brings warmth and light. It is the place of welcoming all things and creating new beginnings. Its light brings illumination and enlightenment. It is the power of knowledge and purification. When acknowledging the East, give thanks for the warmth of the sun and the coming new day. Pray for the revealing light of knowledge.

## 2. South

South is the sun at its highest point. It symbolizes life at its fullest. The southern spirit of the Earth brings gentleness and joy. South brings renewal with the spirit of Earth and life. It is the power of protection and trust. When acknowledging the South, give thanks for the gift of life. Pray for peace in the world.

## 3. West

West is the direction where the sun sets. It symbolizes death. The western spirit of water is the place of dreams, introspection, and the unknown. It signifies purity and strength. Its light symbolizes transformation and healing. When acknowledging the West, give thanks for courage and perseverance. Pray for self-understanding.

## 4. North

North is the direction of darkness. It symbolizes the time of renewal. The northern spirit of the wind brings the power of wisdom. The North is where elders reflect on their lives. When acknowledging the North, give thanks for the wisdom of experience. Pray for the strength to endure hardships.

## 5. Above

Above is the direction of the sun, the moon, the sky, and the cosmos. The sun provides the gift of light, and the moon provides the gravitational pull that moves the waters and the tides of emotion. The sky and the cosmos represent eternity. Above represents the masculine energy of spirit. When acknowledging the Above, give thanks for the creative energies of the universe. Pray for the gift of inspiration.

## 6. Below

Below is the direction of the Earth. The Earth provides the gifts of nature and beauty. Below encompasses all living beings on the planet. Below represents the feminine energy of spirit. When acknowledging the Below, give thanks for the generosity of the Earth. Pray for a true understanding of gratitude.

## 7. Within

Within is the direction of the spirit that exists inside everyone. It provides a connection to all things and encourages humility and respect. Within represents the energy and spirit of the mysterious. When acknowledging the Within, give thanks for your connection with all things. Pray for balance in your life.

# The Seven Reminders

The amount of time you spend practicing reconnecting to the Earth is not necessarily the most important aspect of this process. It is the intent that is the most valuable. Progress can come at any pace. Go at your own speed. Do what you can at the pace your body and mind allow. As you progress, your body will begin to feel the benefits, and your mind will start to open up to a myriad of possibilities. Allow this process to happen naturally. The seven reminders are helpful points to keep in mind as you go.

## 1. Be Patient

It's a long journey and there is no hurry. Things of true value usually take a lot of time to come to maturity. It takes a willingness to wait for things to happen and to be ready when they do. If you commit to the long term, you will not feel pressured to seek quick results. Instead, you can focus on the present moment and allow things to unfold as they are supposed to. Patience will get you a long way.

## 2. Persevere

It is vital to be steady and persistent in your course of action. This is especially true when things get difficult. There will be plenty of obstacles you will have to confront on this journey. Continue regular training of whatever you are able to. Especially try to do something that reflects and strengthens your connection to nature every day. If you miss a day, don't berate yourself; simply do better the next day. Stick to it.

## 3. Do What You're Able

It's not about what you can't do. All you need to do is whatever you can do. No one is going to change the world on their own. Each of us has our own set of skills and abilities. If you simply do what you are able to do with positive intentions and truth in your heart, you will find the way.

## 4. Learn from Everything

Everything that happens to you can be beneficial if you face it with a positive attitude and an open mind. Each experience you have is an opportunity to learn and grow. Everything that happens to you and everyone you meet has something to teach you. Often you may not realize the lesson being imparted, and it will take some thought and quiet reflection to discern the meaning. Sometimes the lesson can be painful with a lasting impact, but if you take your time and contemplate the meaning, all things will become clear.

## 5. Be a Good Teacher

The longer you practice, the more you learn. At some point, you will realize that you have built a wealth of knowledge within you. As you progress, this knowledge will become part of you. Eventually, if you have continued to learn and grow, you will become the teacher. You will recognize lessons you've already learned and be able to pass that knowledge on to others who have not gone through it yet. Once you reach this point, you can begin to help others remember what they already know.

## 6. Be Grateful

Gratitude is an emotion expressing appreciation for what one has, as opposed to what one may want or think they need. Being grateful is living in a reverent state of thanks and acknowledgment for life. It is an attitude that enables a complete conscious connection to the whole. Life is a blessing and all the living beings you encounter are on their own journey. Take a moment to recognize and acknowledge this. There is a life force within all things. Every encounter you have is an opportunity to learn and grow. Give thanks that you recognize this. Be grateful that you have been given this chance to experience life in all its wonder.

## 7. Remember to Breathe

You really should have this one down by now. The more you can remember to breathe during your daily life, the more it becomes a part of you and is available to you when you need it. While it may take years until you are able to consciously breathe deeply as you go about your day, if you start now it will happen.

# The Seven Actions

This handbook has been heading in one direction the whole time. And here we are. If you have made it this far, you are part of it now. It is time to be a living example of the right way to live. It is time to become a caretaker of the Earth. It is time to recognize the necessity of preserving the diversity of the living beings around you. It is time to connect to the whole and reclaim your relationship to nature and yourself. It is your turn to protect the bounty that has surrounded you from the moment you entered the world.

The seven actions are things you can start to do immediately to move forward on this path.

## 1. Unplug

Many people have a fear of nature and being outside. Television, the Internet, and the smart phone have exacerbated this fear. Through the screen, your world is framed within the confines of a small little window. You really have no way of seeing the whole picture, only what is within that window. It is closed in, framed, and comfortable because it is a controlled environment. Prolonged exposure actually makes going outside frightening because outside there is no frame. With the boundaries gone, people who are unfamiliar with nature find it overwhelming. Nature moves from our body outward into the universe. That is a lot to take in if you are used to everything being contained on a screen in your living room.

One of the main culprits of this situation is most definitely commercial television and Internet ads. This kind of advertising is poison to the soul. The flickering images and sound bites are designed to bypass the conscious mind and go directly to the subconscious. If you think you are immune to the effects, you are wrong. Part of the insidiousness of advertisements is that they are designed to resonate on various wavelengths that release chemicals in the brain designed to give pleasure. Everyone enjoys a movie or show sometimes; that is not the issue here. If you have not done it already, it is time to end your relationship with commercial television and learn to avoid advertisements as much as possible. Your mind will thank you.

In addition to unplugging from the television, try to spend at least one day a week away from the computer, the phone, and the Internet. No calls, no e-mails, no Facebook, Twitter, Snapchat, or whatever . . . just leave it alone for a whole day and see if you can notice a vibrational difference.

## 2. Unstuff

We have all felt the pull of stuff. The society we live in promotes the acquisition of more and more and more and more. Acquiring things has the capacity to give us an emotional boost, yet the positive emotions associated with the process are usually quite short lived. Going into debt to buy things you can't afford because you believe your life will be transformed by the purchases is a quick way to unhappiness. Stuff will not fill the emptiness within. It is very difficult not to acquire more stuff. Getting rid of it is a real challenge. Guilt and sentimentality are powerful feelings we attach to many of the things we own. When parents die, it often means that suddenly there's another household of stuff to deal with as well.

The bottom line is that you really don't need all of the stuff that you have. In fact, for many people, stuff has become a huge burden. The stuff you own can begin to feel like you are walking around with ten-pound ankle weights.

The time has come to shed your stuff. Like a snake shedding its skin, you will need to leave behind that which no longer serves a necessary purpose in your life. Give things away. Make donations, give stuff as presents. Do whatever you can to get it out of your life. Unstuff and streamline your being. It can seem like a daunting task, but it is imperative to simplify your life so that you can concentrate on what is truly important.

Begin today. Start to move some of the excess stuff in your life out and away from you. Then sit with the feeling for a while. See if you can notice the change as you lift the burden of stuff from your life and the energy begins to flow.

## 3. Create a Daily Practice

One of the most basic truths in human life is that you become better at something the more you practice it. If you have managed to get this far in this book, you certainly must have some understanding of this concept. Regular practice makes whatever you are doing a part of you. The simple action of doing something repetitively imprints it on your being. Imprinting practices such as meditation, yoga, tai chi, and qigong have a profound effect on who you are.

Begin right now. Stand up. Take a deep breath and move your body. Yes, it takes some discipline. But isn't it time to grow stronger in body, mind, spirit, and soul?

## 4. Connect with Others

When we are interacting with others who feel the same way as we do, we begin to realize we are not alone. There are a lot of people on this path and more are choosing to walk it every day. Feeling the power that is created within a group of like-minded people can be very beneficial. It can help with the process of change. It will begin to heal your heart.

Learning about the things other people are already doing to connect to nature helps bring balance to the knowledge we have about the problems we face. It is not all doom and gloom. You just need to spend time with the right people.

In joining with others, we are taking positive action. Action is the best medicine for navigating the seven stages. Being part of a group means you always have people to share the tasks and provide support. Whether it's by protesting or praying, letter writing, or holding a bake sale for legal fees, we can all do something for the cause of a healthier planet. Our bodies, minds, spirits, and souls will flourish and heal, along with everything we are connected to.

# 5. Learn a New Skill

As the changes taking place on the Earth become more intense, it is vital that you begin to adapt to a different way of living. Those of you who begin now will be that much further along the learning curve by the time the catastrophic system failures begin to be noticed by the general public. As the global economy unravels and cheap imported goods get harder to acquire, it will become imperative to have different options. It might be time to learn to build things with your hands. As our food gets more toxic and expensive, it will be vital to have local alternatives. Start a garden to supplement your food purchases. Learn permaculture, the practice of integrating land, resources, people, and the environment in mutually beneficial ways. As this whole process develops, there will be a rising demand for various tools and technologies that are less complex than what we have become used to. By learning a new skill, you give yourself value in a world where knowledge and ability can make the difference in whether you will be able to survive and thrive during the challenges ahead.

# 6. Give This Book to a Friend

There are many people who can benefit from this handbook. So many people feel lost and adrift in an unfeeling economic system that puts profit above the well-being of people, forests, mountains, rivers, and oceans, and all nonhuman life.

For people struggling with the various addictions and numbing their pain, this handbook can be a guide toward the light. Many people don't realize the effect of the destruction that is taking place around us. It seems normal, yet totally wrong. Reconnecting to nature and the Earth is a healthy alternative to any addiction. Pass this book along to anyone who is struggling with the state of the world.

## 7. Start Your Own Group

When you picked up this book, and began reading, you were acting on feeling or a desire to do something different. Most of us begin this journey alone, growing up in a dying world, where there are more roads than deer paths, more cars than bicycles, more shopping malls than parks or forests, where the sound of birdsongs is drowned out by the roar of traffic, and the starry skies are obliterated by light pollution. You may feel disconnected from nature and from everyone else. The truth is that there are people around you who are aware of the same things; many people feel the same way you do and are ready to get together and do something about it.

By creating a group, you will learn from others and draw strength from being together. You will be with people who want to heal the Earth and reconnect with the Earth as part of their own healing and growth.

For more information on starting your own Reconnecting to the Earth Group please visit our website www.reconnectingtotheearth. com and join the community.

There is no time like the present moment. This may be the end of the book, but it is the beginning of something much greater for you. Go out. Look at the world with a new understanding and begin to feel your connection to the whole. Things will never be the same again.

# Conclusion

*Nature's richness lies in its power to nourish all living things.*
*—I Ching*

There was a lot of concern and consternation leading up to the winter solstice of 2012. According to the Mayan calendar it was the end of a 5,126-year-long cycle. Many held the date as the start of a new period when the Earth and its inhabitants would go through some sort of epic spiritual transformation. Others saw the date as the time of a great catastrophe that would bring about the end of the world. And while there was no epic Hollywood-style cataclysm, the truth is that things have fundamentally shifted since then. Whether you want to attribute the shift to the Mayan calendar or the transition from the Age of Pisces to the Age of Aquarius or any other event or phenomenon, the truth is we are in a time of profound upheaval and change. The changes that are occurring are a result of the continued expansion of the human race and the exploitation of the Earth. We have now simply reached the point where it is becoming clear that we cannot have unlimited growth on a finite planet.

The force of inner truth influences us. If we are quiet enough and able to concentrate our attention within, we can feel when there is something wrong. And there really can be no doubt about this. There is no hiding it any longer. We may not be able to put our finger on it exactly, but it is there. Yet, no matter the darkness we find before us, going through it is the only way to reach the light. It is time for all of us to acknowledge and accept this. Only when we are able to admit something is happening are we able to address the problem.

Reconnecting to the Earth is ultimately an inner journey, yet it leads to the outer reaches of the universe. As we deepen our capacity for direct perception of the world around us, we find that all things are aware, all things are alive, and all things are connected.

Reconnecting to the Earth is a path for returning to the source of human experience and understanding exactly who we are and where we fit into the whole. Contemplation on the meaning underlying the workings of the universe enables us to comprehend the mysterious and divine laws of life and universal truths. This work creates hidden spiritual power that emanates from within and is expressed through everything we do. It is time to transform ordinary actions into manifestations of the sacred.

Be simple in your needs. Be sincere in your interactions with others. Be serene in your state of mind. It is the only path forward.

Namaste.
Peace.

# Recommended Reading

Alexander, Bruce. *The Globalization of Addiction.* Oxford University Press, 2008.

Baker, Carolyn. *Collapsing Consciously: Transformative Truths for Turbulent Times.* North Atlantic Books, 2013.

*Navigating the Coming Chaos: A Handbook for Inner Transition.* IUniverse, 2011.

*Sacred Demise: Walking the Spiritual Path of Industrial Civilization's Collapse.* IUniverse, 2009.

Berry, Thomas. *The Sacred Universe: Earth, Spirituality, and Religion in the 21st Century.* Columbia University Press, 2009.

*Evening Thoughts: Reflecting on Earth as Sacred Community.* Sierra Club Books and University of California Press, 2006.

*The Great Work: Our Way into the Future.* Crown-Bell Publishers (Random House), 1999.

*The Dream of the Earth.* Sierra Club Books, 1988. Reissued 2006.

*Befriending the Earth.* Twenty-third Publications, 1991.

Bird, Christopher, and Peter Tompkins. *The Secret Life of Plants: A Fascinating Account of the Physical, Emotional, and Spiritual Relations between Plants and Man.* Harper & Row, 1989.

Buhner, Stephen Harrod. *Secret Teachings of Plants: The Intelligence of the Heart in the Direct Perception of Nature.* Bear and Company/ Inner Traditions, 2004.

Chopra, Deepak. *The Seven Spiritual Laws of Success.* New World Library, 1994.

Dyer, Wayne. *Your Sacred Self.* HarperCollins, 1995.

Glendinning, Chellis. *My Name Is Chellis and I'm in Recovery from Western Civilization*. Shambhala, 1994.

Greer, John Michael. *The Ecotechnic Future: Envisioning a Post-Peak World*. New Society Publishers, 2009.

*The Long Descent: A User's Guide to the End of the Industrial Age*. New Society Publishers, 2008.

Hoopes, Aaron. *Breathe Smart: The Secret to Happiness, Health and Long Life,* 2nd edition. Zen Yoga Press, 2008.

*Perfecting Ourselves: Coordinating Body, Mind and Spirit*. Turtle Press, 2002.

*Zen Yoga: A Path to Enlightenment through Breathing, Movement and Meditation*. Kodansha International, 2007.

Kunstler, James Howard. *The Long Emergency: Surviving the Converging Catastrophes of the Twenty-First Century*. Grove/Atlantic, 2005.

Louv, Richard. *Last Child in the Woods: Saving Our Children from Nature-Deficit Disorder*. Algonquin Books, 2008.

Plotkin, Bill. *Nature and the Human Soul: Cultivating Wholeness and Community in a Fragmented World*. New World Library, 2008.

*Soulcraft: Crossing into the Mysteries of Nature and Psyche*. New World Library, 2003.

Tzu, Lao, and Stephen Mitchell. *The Tao Te Ching*. Harper Perennial, 1992.

Watts, Alan. *The Book: On the Taboo against Knowing Who You Are*. Pantheon Books, 1966.

# About the Author

**Aaron Hoopes** (BA, Japanese culture and language, E-RYT500) has studied karate, kung fu, tai chi, qigong, and yoga for over thirty-five years. A native of Vermont, he spent many years in Japan and Australia studying with a number of exceptional teachers. He is the founder of Zen Yoga and the author of numerous books including *Zen Yoga: A Path to Enlightenment through Breathing, Movement and Meditation*; *Perfecting Ourselves: Coordinating Body, Mind and Spirit*; *Breathe Smart: The Secret to Happiness, Health and Long Life*; and *The Zen Anti-Diet*. His best-selling *Zen Yoga Daily Warm-Up* DVD has helped thousands of people integrate breathing and gentle movement into their lives. He is a Zen Shiatsu massage therapist and a longtime student of permaculture and plant spirit medicine. He runs the Dragon Mountain Kung Fu School and teaches yoga and qigong classes at the Zen Mountain Healing Center in Vermont. Visit him online at www.zenmountainhealing.com.

For more information about Zen Yoga, please visit www.artofzenyoga.com.

# Books by Aaron Hoopes

### Reconnecting To The Earth
Published by: Ozark Mountain Publishing

### Update: Japan
Published by: Intercultural Press 1998

### Perfecting Ourselves: Coordinating Body, Mind and Spirit
Published by: Turtle Press 2002

### Breathe Smart: The Secret to Happiness, Health and Long Life
Published by: Zen Yoga Press, 2003, **2nd Edition**, 2008

### Inner Sunrise Guided Meditation CD
Published by: Zen Yoga Press, 2004

### Zen Yoga Daily Warm-Up DVD
Published by: Zen Yoga Press, 2006

### Zen Yoga: The Path to Enlightenment through Breathing, Movement and Meditation
Published by: Kodansha International, 2007

For more information about any of the above titles, soon to be released titles, or other items in our catalog, write, phone or visit our website:
Ozark Mountain Publishing, Inc.
PO Box 754, Huntsville, AR 72740
479-738-2348/800-935-0045
www.ozarkmt.com

# If you liked this book, you might also like:

*Heaven Here on Earth*
by Curt Melliger
*The Old is New*
*L.R. Sumpter*
*Imagining the Unimaginable*
by Richard Rowe
*Raising Our Vibrations for the New Age*
*By Sherri Cortland*
*Coming Home to Lemuria*
*By Charmain Redwood*

For more information about any of the above titles, soon to be released titles,
or other items in our catalog, write, phone or visit our website:
Ozark Mountain Publishing, Inc.
PO Box 754, Huntsville, AR 72740
479-738-2348
www.ozarkmt.com

# Other Books by Ozark Mountain Publishing, Inc.

**Dolores Cannon**
A Soul Remembers Hiroshima
Between Death and Life
Conversations with Nostradamus,
    Volume I, II, III
The Convoluted Universe -Book One,
    Two, Three, Four, Five
The Custodians
Five Lives Remembered
Jesus and the Essenes
Keepers of the Garden
Legacy from the Stars
The Legend of Starcrash
The Search for Hidden Sacred Knowledge
They Walked with Jesus
The Three Waves of Volunteers and the
    New Earth
**Aron Abrahamsen**
Holiday in Heaven
Out of the Archives – Earth Changes
**Justine Alessi & M. E. McMillan**
Rebirth of the Oracle
**Kathryn/Patrick Andries**
Naked in Public
**Kathryn Andries**
The Big Desire
Dream Doctor
Soul Choices: Six Paths to Find Your Life
    Purpose
Soul Choices: Six Paths to Fulfilling
    Relationships
**Patrick Andries**
Owners Manual for the Mind
**Dan Bird**
Finding Your Way in the Spiritual Age
Waking Up in the Spiritual Age
**Julia Cannon**
Soul Speak – The Language of Your Body
**Ronald Chapman**
Seeing True
**Albert Cheung**
The Emperor's Stargate
**Jack Churchward**
Lifting the Veil on the Lost Continent of
    Mu
The Stone Tablets of Mu
**Sherri Cortland**
Guide Group Fridays
Raising Our Vibrations for the New Age

Spiritual Tool Box
Windows of Opportunity
**Patrick De Haan**
The Alien Handbook
**Paulinne Delcour-Min**
Spiritual Gold
**Michael Dennis**
Morning Coffee with God
God's Many Mansions
**Carolyn Greer Daly**
Opening to Fullness of Spirit
**Anita Holmes**
Twidders
**Aaron Hoopes**
Reconnecting to the Earth
**Victoria Hunt**
Kiss the Wind
**Patricia Irvine**
In Light and In Shade
**Kevin Killen**
Ghosts and Me
**Diane Lewis**
From Psychic to Soul
**Donna Lynn**
From Fear to Love
**Maureen McGill**
Baby It's You
**Maureen McGill & Nola Davis**
Live from the Other Side
**Curt Melliger**
Heaven Here on Earth
**Henry Michaelson**
And Jesus Said – A Conversation
**Dennis Milner**
Kosmos
**Andy Myers**
Not Your Average Angel Book
**Guy Needler**
Avoiding Karma
Beyond the Source – Book 1, Book 2
The Anne Dialogues
The Curators
The History of God
The Origin Speaks
**James Nussbaumer**
And Then I Knew My Abundance
The Master of Everything
Mastering Your Own Spiritual Freedom

For more information about any of the above titles, soon to be released titles,
or other items in our catalog, write, phone or visit our website:
PO Box 754, Huntsville, AR 72740
479-738-2348/800-935-0045
www.ozarkmt.com

# Other Books by Ozark Mountain Publishing, Inc.

**Sherry O'Brian**
Peaks and Valleys
**Riet Okken**
The Liberating Power of Emotions
**Gabrielle Orr**
Akashic Records: One True Love
Let Miracles Happen
**Victor Parachin**
Sit a Bit
**Nikki Pattillo**
A Spiritual Evolution
Children of the Stars
**Rev. Grant H. Pealer**
A Funny Thing Happened on the
    Way to Heaven
Worlds Beyond Death
**Victoria Pendragon**
Born Healers
Feng Shui from the Inside, Out
Sleep Magic
The Sleeping Phoenix
**Michael Perlin**
Fantastic Adventures in Metaphysics
**Walter Pullen**
Evolution of the Spirit
**Debra Rayburn**
Let's Get Natural with Herbs
**Charmian Redwood**
A New Earth Rising
Coming Home to Lemuria
**David Rivinus**
Always Dreaming
**Richard Rowe**
Imagining the Unimaginable
**M. Don Schorn**
Elder Gods of Antiquity
Legacy of the Elder Gods
Gardens of the Elder Gods
Reincarnation...Stepping Stones of Life
**Garnet Schulhauser**
Dance of Eternal Rapture
Dance of Heavenly Bliss

Dancing Forever with Spirit
Dancing on a Stamp
**Manuella Stoerzer**
Headless Chicken
**Annie Stillwater Gray**
Education of a Guardian Angel
The Dawn Book
Work of a Guardian Angel
**Blair Styra**
Don't Change the Channel
Who Catharted
**Natalie Sudman**
Application of Impossible Things
**L.R. Sumpter**
Judy's Story
The Old is New
We Are the Creators
**Jim Thomas**
Tales from the Trance
**Nicholas Vesey**
Living the Life-Force
**Janie Wells**
Embracing the Human Journey
Payment for Passage
**Dennis Wheatley/ Maria Wheatley**
The Essential Dowsing Guide
**Maria Wheatley**
Druidic Soul Star Astrology
**Jacquelyn Wiersma**
The Zodiac Recipe
**Sherry Wilde**
The Forgotten Promise
**Lyn Willmoth**
A Small Book of Comfort
**Stuart Wilson & Joanna Prentis**
Atlantis and the New Consciousness
Beyond Limitations
The Essenes -Children of the Light
The Magdalene Version
Power of the Magdalene
**Robert Winterhalter**
The Healing Christ

For more information about any of the above titles, soon to be released titles,
or other items in our catalog, write, phone or visit our website:
PO Box 754, Huntsville, AR 72740
479-738-2348/800-935-0045
www.ozarkmt.com